The Common Ground:

Political Issues Facing America

Second Edition

By: Chandler Rivinius

Dedication

To my Creator, who was gracious enough to provide me with free time to spend writing and to my family who supported me in this endeavor even though this most likely seemed like a fool's errand.

Table of Contents

Acknowledgments

Writing is not a skill that I am naturally inclined to. This book was very much a proof of concept as well as a grand challenge for me as an individual. With that being the case, I would like to thank my parents and siblings for their encouragement during the whole process. I would also like to thank all the teachers and professors who have provided me with the knowledge, skills, and experiences that have shaped me into the person I am today. I would like to give special thanks to my high school English teacher, whose efforts made the most significant contribution towards making me a semi-competent writer.

Second Edition Commentary: About 16 million written words later, you can certainly tell how much difference a bit of practice makes. My domain of excellence is still math, but I've managed to achieve a degree of literary competence.

"So in everything, do to others what you would have them do to you, for this sums up the Law and the Prophets." Matthew 7:12 (NIV)

"Therefore everyone who hears these words of mine and puts them into practice is like a wise man who built his house on the rock. The rain came down, the streams rose, and the winds blew and beat against that house; yet it did not fall, because it had its foundation on the rock." Matthew 7:24-25 (NIV)

"If a house is divided against itself, that house cannot stand." Mark 3:25 (NIV)

Preface

My intention for this book is to provide an overview of a few of the issues facing America these days (2018-19). I hope to do this in such a way that everyone can easily understand these issues. I took the time to put this together to promote unity and to shed light on the fact that as Americans, the things we share in common with each other outnumber the things that make us different.

For each issue, the format selected for this overview will include providing relevant background information with appropriate sources for the intended scope. This background information will be followed by the stances of the two largest political parties in America along with some of the respective justifications provided by each. Each issue will then be concluded with some commonsense compromises that the majority of Americans should be able to agree upon.

I am going to attempt writing all of this in an unbiased fashion. I fully expect this attempt to fail at some points, as it is impossible to completely eliminate one's own bias. With that said, I currently adhere to predominantly conservative views in most policy matters. I will make every effort to ensure that this bias is expressed as little as possible. Objectivity will be one of the primary points of focus for this book. This is to ensure that all readers can feel like they are welcome at the table.

As a final note, this book is not intended to encompass every issue that is currently facing America. I have selected the items that have been most prevalent and persisting over the last couple of years. This selection does not mean that there are no compromises available for the excluded issues. When viewed objectively, readers will find that an understanding can be reached more often than not for nearly all disagreements.

More than anything, the issue selection here reflects a certain degree of time availability. Given infinite time, I would endeavor to tackle all of the issues facing the American people, but unfortunately, such an undertaking is not presently possible as my free time is limited. It is also important to note that I am human and therefore prone to making errors. Mistakes can and will most likely occur in this book. As time goes on, I will correct as many of them as I can.

To make this book more friendly to the common man, I limited my use of citations and source material to the facts and background sections on each issue. Issue by issue views for each party will be referenced as well and the source provided, however, the analysis and explanations will be my own and in my own words.

At the end of the day, when all things are said and done, the best way to view this book is as a timesaver. This book encompasses nine topics that are facing the United States right now. These nine topics will also most likely continue to be a problem in the United States for the foreseeable future. It took roughly 150 hours to gather the relevant research on all of these topics and many more hours to organize them into this format. I am by no means an expert in hunting down sources, but I did survive college back in the day and have at least average competence in source-hunting.

The final word count is somewhere around 38,000. The average adult has a reading speed of approximately 250 words per minute. Since that is the average speed, there is a decent chance that most people can read faster. However, using the average adult reading speed, it would take a person about three hours to read through this whole book. At that speed, reading this book has the effect of allowing someone to condense nearly four work weeks of political issue research into a single evening of reading.

I hope that this book can provide many people with some of the benefits that accompany a better understanding of the issues we will discuss. All while saving everyone who reads it a substantial amount of time. With any luck, the people who take the time to read this will be able to spend the time this book saved them with their family or engaged in other activities that they enjoy. For this book, I focused on using reliable sources but also readily available. My goal was to use sources that a reasonable person would most likely find and use if they were to endeavor to investigate these issues on their own time. As a result, not all of the sources are of scientific journal quality. With that said, hopefully, the sources I have selected are adequately close to the level of accuracy that the task requires. It is also my hope that those who read this enjoy it and that it adds some value to their lives.

Second Edition Commentary:

An opportunity presented itself to release this as well as A Young Adult's Guide To Life (AYAGTL), in a hardcover format. After discussing the matter with the editorial team, we decided that it makes sense to add a bit of content and call it a second edition since we're going to do a cover refresh as well. This is part of a larger effort to bring all my creative works under the Chandler Rivinius name.

Both The Common Ground: Political Issues Facing America (TCGPIFA) and AYAGTL were published using the C. Rivinius pen name. The idea behind that was to partition my non-fiction works from my fictional works using a different pen name. This was to prevent any blowback from my nonfiction writing affecting my fiction writing.

However, the benefits of hindsight reveal that it's more efficient to keep everything under the same umbrella. The multi name, same author scheme has only been a source of confusion. As I get older, I also care less and less about blowback. Writing is a hobby for me. One of many. Therefore, it makes sense to streamline the process and make it enjoyable.

Beyond that, this second edition contains very little new content. Just some commentary at the end of each section. In said commentary, I'll basically comment on how well the material has aged in the last four years. After having written both nonfiction and fiction, I've come to abhor nonfiction writing. This is based on the grounds that it's a pain in the butt. Nothing messes up a flow state quite as much as having to stop to cite sources and all that bunk.

Writing the Swift City Chronicles and the Voyage of the Pervicacious was a much more pleasant experience. However, nonfiction does have the redeeming quality of being real and being useful. So, we'll see if I ever make my way back to it again someday. If I do, I'll have to find a way around the bibliography or something like that. At any rate, let's dive into the second edition.

Chapter 1: The Fundamental Principle of Open Dialogue

Before we can begin looking into the issues discussed in the following pages, we must first explore the common ground on which we stand. I think the miracle of human life is the best place for us to start. Life is something that we all share, and something we all have some degree of personal experience with. With that being said, on the topic of human life, my claim is this: Life is all about making decisions. It may seem like a bold claim, but it is a claim that I think holds true.

These decisions range from how we choose to spend our time, to how we choose to spend our money. Almost everything we do involves one of these two things. Many of us decide to convert our time into money daily through work. Some of us have enough money to allow us to choose not to work, which is effectively buying back time. Regardless, how we choose to spend our time and money is ultimately what determines who we are and where we are at in life.

For example, you took a left turn instead of a right turn at the last stop light, and now you are outside of your favorite coffee shop. You decided to go to college for a degree in engineering instead of joining the air force, and now you have an office job that keeps you far away from the clouds. You decided to work hard at the gym every day for a whole month, and now you are 7 pounds lighter and much stronger than you were before. All three of these examples illustrate how decisions we make every day are used to build our futures. To borrow from the Iron Giant, we are very much who we choose to be. We build ourselves with our decisions, and this is of fundamental importance.

I think this very same principle can be scaled up to describe how something like our nation works as well. Since individuals make up households, households make up neighborhoods, neighborhoods make up cities, cities make up states, and states make up nations, it can be inferred that the fate of a country is determined through the same process of consecutive decision making. That is to say, just like people, nations are built by their decisions as well.

We, as citizens of a nation, rely on our government to make the consecutive decisions that are required to guide our nation. A common misconception is that our country is a democracy. This is not quite the case. In a democracy, each citizen votes directly on the issues at hand to guide the course of their nation. This works well in a small setting, but this fails when put into practice on a large scale. As the number of voting individuals in a democracy increases, the number of issues and concerns increases as well. All of these new issues need to be considered, and the situation quickly turns into a mess.

In the case of a vast nation such as the United States, direct democracy would be almost impossible since there would be hundreds of thousands of issues to consider. Given the size of our country, many of these issues would be regional and therefore only affect certain groups of people. Having a system like this would be a substantial misuse of time for everyone involved. A farmer in Nebraska could end up voting on speed limits in Florida. A professor in New York could end up voting on Washington state commercial fishing regulations. If they are intelligent and well informed, both the professor and the farmer most likely will manage to vote alright in these examples. With that said, taking the time to vote on these issues and everything in between would take up a massive amount of time that both the farmer and the professor could spend doing something more productive. By avoiding a direct democracy, this time can then be spent on pursuits more closely related to their respective interests.

Multiple layers of representative democracy could be used to address the issue of too many issues. However, this would have some issues of its own, and our founding fathers devised a more elegant solution. To avoid wasting time and for a few other reasons such as preventing tyranny, the founding fathers of the United States selected a representative republic as our form of government instead of an outright direct democracy.

To be entirely factually correct, a federal presidential constitutional republic was selected as our form of government. The use of a republic allows individuals to elect officials to vote on their behalf. This saves us time at the cost of our direct say in the decisions that are made on our behalf. Using a gross simplification, our federal presidential constitutional republic means that we are a group of states, bound together by a constitution, who have elected a president along with representatives to govern us.

A consequence of our system is that we now find ourselves in a situation where we need to persuade others to agree with us for action to take place. This is where difficulties arise since we do not all share the same circumstances, and subsequently, we do not all benefit from the same collective decisions. On top of this, as a general rule, we also have a tendency to look out for our own personal interests first.

This situation can be simplified down to a case where there are only two parties. At a basic level when action is required and two parties co-exist that have to make decisions together, there are only two possible outcomes that can take place. Either the parties will agree, or the parties will disagree. The parties could also choose a third, neutral option, but since choosing the neutral option would result in a state of inaction, we can just disregard it and go back to assuming there are only two choices. In the first of our two cases, agreement occurs, and the decision is made, and matters can move forward to the next item of business. In the second of our two cases, disagreement occurs, a gridlock is reached, and no forward progress can be made until a resolution is found. This would not be an unsatisfactory arrangement if both cases occurred half of the time. But unfortunately, in realistic situations, a 50-50 split is not usually the outcome we end up with.

In practice sometimes we manage to reach agreements whereas other times we are lucky if we agree on anything at all.

With a situation like this being the current state of affairs in our country the only way to work cooperatively with each other is to be able to use open dialogue to find a way to work out differences and reach an agreement that is satisfactory to both parties involved. By open dialogue, I am referring to the process of two parties coming together, creating an environment in which everyone feels safe, and then openly and honestly discussing their differences to work things out. This working out of differences is the act of reaching a compromise. In a two-party system, such as the federal presidential constitutional republic found here in the United States, compromise is the key to getting anything done. As one might have deduced from the prior statement, the only way to reach a compromise is through the use of open dialogue with the opposing party. Without this dialogue, an agreement cannot be reached, and progress towards a decision cannot be made. It is at this point that the immense importance of having an open dialogue between the opposing parties becomes crystal clear. If we choose not to communicate with the parties holding different viewpoints than our own, we will never be able to make any forward progress.

This is very much the state that we currently find much of the United States in. Or rather this is at least the state that many individuals believe the United States to be in. In reality, our situation is not as grim as it seems. We have a large number of people who are not talking to each other. We also have a component of people who talk to each other rather violently. Both of these situations are not helpful, but fortunately, there is hope. The political views and the feelings of Americans regarding the issues facing the United States most likely fall along a normal distribution curve. That is to say, the majority of Americans probably do not entirely support either side of an issue. Instead, the majority of Americans probably hold moderate viewpoints.

Since moderate viewpoints are considered boring and uninteresting, they are often overlooked in favor of the more extreme views that are held by a much smaller component of the population. These extreme viewpoints are often debated and, in many ways, promoted by the media to the general population. It is this false representation that leads to a belief that those who identify as being part of the opposing party also hold the most extreme views of that party and are therefore not fit to associate with.

Most often, this belief is entirely incorrect, and further inspection will reveal that we share more in common with the majority of people in the opposing party than we would ever begin to imagine. The misconception that everyone in the opposing party is awful leads to a significant misunderstanding. This misunderstanding is one of the primary sources of the division that we find in our country today. The key to repairing this division is seen through the use of open dialogue with one another in our interactions. Through dialogue, we can reach the understanding that we have more in common with each other than we think and that our differences are often small in comparison.

To reach this understanding, there is a significant difficulty that we must overcome. Open dialogue can sometimes invoke a feeling of being under attack within us. As human beings, we have a tendency to identify with the views we hold and to use these views as part of what we consider to be our own identity. Our views allow us to feel like we are part of a group. This channels our tribal mentality from days long past, and it triggers powerful instincts within us. As a result, when these views are under attack, it can feel like we are also under attack. As part of our nature, flight or fight is triggered. We immediately take defensive action and close our minds to new ideas. Whether we do this by avoidance or by getting angry and pushing back, the end result is the same. We do this to protect ourselves from the damage that might occur to our identity if we re-examine our views. This is essentially using our bias towards our own views as a shield against new views, with views that are similar to our own serving to strengthen our shield through confirmation bias.

As a result of this, it is very beneficial for us to begin to think about our views as being objects that we can collect and upgrade as opposed to being a part of our identity. It is also beneficial to view ourselves as individuals and not part of a group. This approach allows us to have a separation between who we are and what we believe. The result of this separation is that we now can debate the thoughts and the ideas that make up our views without feeling like we are being attacked or scrutinized.

Taking the proactive approach of seeking out the best ideas based on their merits when compared to other ideas has the effect of elevating our thinking and discourse to a much higher level than what we currently find in our society. The whole process can be compared to panning for gold in a river. The ideas that have more merit are dense and located at the bottom of the pan, but they are mixed in with less dense ideas and ideas of lesser quality. Only washing the ideas with the waters of debate and reflection can carry away the less dense and lower quality ideas, leaving the best and most valuable ideas at the bottom of the pan.

It is precisely for this purpose that we need to be willing to openly talk to each other and listen to the ideas of others. Even if we choose not to adopt these ideas, the very act of listening to different ideas can help us to sort through and refine our own ideas into ideas of higher quality. It should be the goal of every individual to have the highest quality ideas that they can find. If an individual is exposed to an idea that he or she can rationally evaluate the individual should always make that evaluation. If that idea is determined to possess more merit than any of the current ideas that the individual has, he or she should elect to adopt this new idea for his or her own until a new idea with even more merit is found.

The failure to take the approach of continually trying to find the best idea can be seen everywhere in America at the time of writing this book. The unexpected presidential victory in the 2016 election could partly be a result of a good portion of the population feeling under attack for the ideas that they held. As opposed to explaining why the ideas of these people held less merit, many media sources chose to directly attack the individuals who held these ideas by giving them offensive labels.

This attacking of the individuals and not of the ideas that the individuals hold is precisely the sort of action that leads to more division and negative interactions between those involved. Recalling the normal distribution that many people fall on, many of the individuals who reside in the middle of the curve were possibly polarized by the abuse heaped on them, and thus much more likely to vote for the candidate who was attacking their views less.

Since the current model of our civil discourse is not the one described above, the next question is "How do we get from where we currently are, to this place where we consider the opinions of others without attacking them or feeling under attack ourselves?". The answer to this question is that we must remember that at the end of the day, we are all Americans. The actions and circumstances that benefit one of us will benefit all of us to a certain degree. We must remember that as a society, the number of things we have in common is more significant than our differences. We have common needs that must be met, and we all have similar desires in life. To name a few of these common desires: we all want to breathe air, we all want to eat our fill of food, we all want to drink clean water when we are thirsty, we all want to be able to use roads to travel around, and we all want enough space to live in. Our common desires aside, we have many other things in common. Of these common things, perhaps most fundamentally, we are all 99.9% genetically similar to one another [1]. With this commonality in mind, the people we view as the "enemy" are as human as we are, having similar needs, similar wants, and similar desires. At the end of the day, we really do need to be our brother's keeper.

As we discuss the issues in the following chapters, we should try our best to adopt this mindset: fellow Americans are friends, not enemies, regardless of political affiliation. If not taken permanently, then this mindset should at least be used for the duration of time we choose to spend on the topics of this book. Our goal here is to have an open dialogue about each of these issues and to broaden our understanding of the situation as a whole.

If nothing else, by the time the last chapter is reached, we should have a better understanding of the underlying background related to each issue. This information should be of value in any upcoming discussions you might have with people you would consider to be of the opposing side, however hopefully after reading this introductory chapter, you realize that the opposite side is not so much an enemy as they are a wayward brother. Now let us begin.

Second Edition Commentary:

Much to my surprise, this first chapter aged well. I can tell that my writing style could certainly use a bit of work but beyond that, the content is still valid. Now, just as back then, we still have more in common with each other than we realize.

Chapter 2: The Issue of Abortion

Background:

We shall start our discussion with the issue of abortion. The term abortion refers to the medical process of ending a pregnancy through the removal of the fetus or embryo before survival outside of the uterus is possible. The term abortion is also used interchangeably to describe the termination of a late-term pregnancy in which the fetus could potentially survive outside of the uterus. An unintentional, unassisted abortion is referred to as a miscarriage. Those would be the primary terms related to abortion, so with the terminology aside, in the case of intentional abortion, two primary means are used to accomplish the removal of the fetus. These two means are chemical removal or surgical removal. We will discuss the chemical means of removal first.

Having a chemical abortion is the best-case scenario for a woman who wishes to terminate her pregnancy. Certain chemicals can be used in the early stages of pregnancy to initiate a chemical abortion. Chemical abortion methods usually rely on creating a hormonal environment that is unsuitable for the survival of the fetus. In this case, the fetus is broken down by the body and passed out of the body via blood flow. This method of abortion is the least intrusive for the patient undergoing the procedure. Chemical abortions are also referred to as a medical abortion since abortion chemicals are ingested in the form of oral medicine. We will use this terminology going forward. The risk of death associated with a medical abortion to terminate a pregnancy within the first 63 days of gestation is 1/100,000 [2].

Medical abortion aside, the other primary method to perform an abortion is through the use of surgical means to remove the fetus. As one might have guessed, this is known as a surgical abortion. Surgical abortions are more common in the later stages of pregnancy. This is a result of the fact that medical abortion methods begin to lose their effectiveness as the pregnancy progresses. The procedures for a surgical abortion are more invasive for patients and are often associated with a certain degree of discomfort. The risk of death related to having a surgical abortion performed in the first 63 days of gestation is around 1/1,000,000 [3]. Similar to surgical abortion, there is also a dilatation and evacuation abortion method. This method is most common when a surgical abortion would no longer be effective. Like a surgical abortion, this dilatation and evacuation procedure is also invasive when performed on a patient. The risk of death increases with the length of the pregnancy, so an exact risk of death is not readily available. To put the risk factors I mentioned above in perspective, the risk of death associated with giving birth, in general, is roughly around 17.3/100,000 [4].

The total number of abortions reported for the year 2014 by the Center for Disease Control and Prevention was 652,639 [5]. From the same source over the same period, the abortion rate was 12.1 per 1000 women in the 15-44 age range. There were 186 abortions for every 1000 live births [5]. Younger women accounted for a higher component of abortions with women aged 20-24 accounting for 32.2% and women aged 25-29 accounting for 26.7% of the abortions that were reported [5]. Women aged 15-19 accounted for 10.4% of the abortions that were reported [5].

Overall, the abortion rate has been decreasing. For example, the current abortion rate for the women in the 15-19 age range reduced by 49% when compared to the 2005 rate [5]. The majority of abortions were performed before the 8th week after gestation, with about 67% of abortions being performed before that mark [5]. 91.5% of abortions were performed within 13 weeks of gestation [5]. 7.2% were performed between the 14th and 20th week, and about 1.3% of abortions were performed after 21 weeks [5].

22.6% of abortions were medical abortions, and about 67.4% were surgical abortions performed before the 13th week [5].

8.6% were surgical abortions performed 13 weeks or more after gestation [5]. The remaining 1.4% of abortions were performed with uncommon methods [5]. All these percentages can seem a bit abstract, so to provide some additional perspective, the 1.3% of abortions performed after 21 weeks translates into about 8,484 abortions when using the 2014 total number of abortions as our reference point. With that, we can wrap up our abortion rate background section and move on to our next section, abortion law.

As far as the law is concerned, the U.S. Supreme Court Roe v. Wade case in 1973 affirmed the constitutional right for women to have abortions. The Planned Parenthood v. Casey case in 1992 also ruled that an "undue burden" cannot be placed on women seeking an abortion. In 1977 the Hyde Amendment prohibited the use of federal funds to pay for abortions except in cases where the procedure would be performed to save the life of the mother or to terminate a pregnancy that resulted from rape or incest. The individuals primarily affected by the Hyde Amendment are those that rely on Medicare for their health coverage. The Hyde Amendment only applies to federal spending, allowing states to spend money in support of abortions if they choose to.

At a state level, 12 states appear to be supportive of abortion rights, and 29 states appear to be hostile toward abortion rights [6]. The remaining states have not taken a hard stance on the issue of abortion. The qualifying factor for being considered a hostile abortion state is having restrictions in place that make abortions challenging to obtain. For our purposes, we will not dive into the state-by-state laws that regulate abortion. Instead, we will finish up by looking into the cost and insurance coverage of abortions.

Regarding insurance coverage and the cost for an abortion, many insurance providers either do not cover abortions or the coverage is only included under specific plans. Of the woman who had an abortion in 2014 and reported insurance data, 31%

had private insurance, and 35% had Medicaid coverage although these statistics do not indicate that the procedures were covered by insurance [6]. Of the women who had abortions in 2014, 53% paid for the abortion out of pocket [6]. In 2014 the second most common method of payment after paying out of pocket was Medicaid in the states that provided Medicaid funding for abortions [6]. Medicaid was followed by private insurance [6]. The average amount paid for a surgical abortion was $508, and the average amount paid for medical abortion was $535 [6].

This represents a substantial amount of money, especially for women of lower socioeconomic status. With the conclusion of this paragraph, we have covered the basics of abortion terminology, methodology, abortion rates, abortion laws, and abortion costs. We can now discuss the stances of our political parties.

The Stance on the Left: Pro-choice

Starting with the older of the two parties, according to their 2012 party platform, the Democratic Party supports the Roe v. Wade decision and the right of a woman to make decisions regarding her pregnancy regardless of her ability to pay. They oppose efforts to weaken this right or to undermine it. According to this platform, the Democratic Party holds that abortion is a personal decision of a woman, her family, her doctor, and her clergy. The platform states that there is no place for politicians or the government to get in the way of and interfere with a woman and her right to make decisions regarding her body. The Democratic Party recognizes that healthcare and education reduce the number of unintended pregnancies and reduce the need for abortions. They support a woman's decision to have a child by providing affordable health care and ensuring the availability of and access to programs that help women during pregnancy and after the birth of a child, including adoption programs [7].

Many lines of reasoning are used in support of the pro-choice stance. One of the more major supporting reasons in favor of the pro-choice position is provided by the impact that pregnancy can have on a woman's life. A common argument is that a woman should not be solely responsible for the consequences of an action that she committed with a partner. If the man responsible for impregnating her has the option to leave her, then she should not be stuck with the responsibility of raising their child alone.

Arguments similar to this more or less stem back to an underlying argument that the processes of pregnancy, childbirth and the raising of children are a burden on women and that these processes put women at a disadvantage when compared to men. The burden of pregnancy, childbirth, and raising a child also serves as a basis for another common argument in favor of pro-choice. Having a child is a 9-month commitment that involves physical changes, suffering through the actual birth of the child, and then the time consuming and financially taxing efforts that go into raising a child after the birth takes place. This process is life changing. It can force a woman to put a lot of other areas in her life on hold. Her education or her career are both areas that can suffer. It is clear that the potential cost is not only measured in dollars but also in missed opportunities. The point of contention is that forcing a woman to undergo this level of sacrifice is unreasonable and wrong.

Another point related to the impact pregnancy has on a woman's life is that childbirth is excruciating and potentially fatal. The odds of dying from giving birth are much higher than the odds of winning the lottery or getting struck by lightning in a given year. This point in and of itself serves as the justification for having an abortion since it carries less risk than childbirth.

Moving away from arguments that are based on the impact having a child has on the potential mother, there are also arguments to support pro-choice based on the idea that abortion is doing an unborn child a favor. This line of reasoning states that if the mother chooses to go through with a pregnancy begrudgingly and has the child, that child will be unwanted and a source of resentment for the mother. The idea then is that it would have been better for that child to have never been born than to come into a world where the child's sole caregiver does not care for it.

Another argument similar to this is that if the mother is unable to provide for the child then once again the child would be better off not being born at all than living a life that started in poverty. Also related to this is the idea that never being born is different from dying, and therefore, an abortion does not amount to killing a child.

Other pro-choice arguments are based more on political ideology and ideas as opposed to concern for the mother and potential child. One such argument for pro-choice comes from the concept of limited government with liberty for all. In the case of liberty for all, the argument becomes the idea that people should be able to do what they want. For the case of limited government, the reasoning is that the government should not have the authority to tell a woman what she can or cannot do with her body. In some cases, this argument is tied to the feminist movement by changing the phrase "government" to the phrase "patriarchy."

In this case, the idea changes from merely being against government interference, to being against having people who cannot identify with having an abortion, creating the policy that governs abortions. More concisely, since the patriarchy typically does not have experience with being poor or with having abortions, they are not qualified to make laws that deal with abortions.

Overall, these three branches make up the majority of the argument for pro-choice, but they are by no means an all-encompassing tree of the arguments in support of pro-choice. Some smaller points are used to counter specific opposition points. To run through some of these, one common argument for abortion over adoption is that the adoption process is very time consuming and potentially costly. Related to this is the argument that just giving birth to a baby is an expensive process, and that abortion is a good alternative for those who cannot afford it.

Another common argument used when abortion is compared to murder is to state that a fetus is not viable outside of the mother's body and is, therefore, nothing more than a mass of cells. In some cases, it has been argued that a fetus is not much different than a parasite. Other fringe arguments have been made that link abortion to a reduced crime rate or classify abortion as a viable method of population control. All of these examples are a bit on the fringe side of things.

As a final remark and disclaimer, the arguments listed above do not represent all of the arguments that exist in favor of pro-choice. The arguments that have been discussed are merely some of the arguments that are more popular when the topic of abortion is debated. At an individual level, many members of the Democratic Party may not support or believe all of the arguments mentioned above or even wholly support the Democratic Party platform for that matter. It is worth noting that in many cases, supporters of the pro-choice stance are not actually supporters of abortion and the termination of a fetus. They are just supporters of the right for women to have that option of abortion available to them. Hence the pro-choice label.

The Stance on the Right: Pro-Life

Moving on to the other party, according to their 2012 party platform, the Republican Party is faithful to the "self-evident" truths enshrined in the Declaration of Independence. The Republican Party believes in the sanctity of human life. It follows that they also think that an unborn child has a fundamental individual right to life. To that end, the Republican Party supports a human life amendment to the Constitution. They support legislation to make it clear that the Fourteenth Amendment's protections also apply to unborn children. The Republican Party is opposed to using public revenues to promote or perform abortions or to fund organizations that perform or advocate for abortions. The Republican Party does not want to support or subsidize any health care options that include abortion coverage.

They support the appointment of judges who respect traditional family values and believe in the sanctity of innocent human life. The Republican Party opposes the non-consensual withholding or withdrawal of care or treatment, including food and water, from people with disabilities, including newborns, as well as the elderly and infirm. They also oppose active and passive euthanasia and assisted suicide. [8] This more or less covers the Republican Party stance on abortion.

As with pro-choice, many lines of reasoning can be used in support of the pro-life stance. The primary line of supportive reasoning is that abortion amounts to the murder of innocent unborn children. This statement can be justified a few different ways. The first pillar of the argument is usually based on the idea that from the moment of conception, a new human being is brought into existence. This newly created existence is accepted to be fully alive and fully human with all of the inalienable rights that come with being human. It is at this point that the argument tends to vary.

From the perspective of the constitution, the argument is that the first section of the 14th Amendment deems it unlawful for the state to deprive any person of life, liberty, or property without due process of the law. Therefore because of this, it would then be unlawful to deprive this newly formed person of his or her life. The same argument from a moral perspective is that it is generally accepted that the taking of another person's life is wrong. Since this is wrong, then taking the life of an unborn child is also wrong and amounts to murder. A slight twist on this argument relies on the Unborn Victims of Violence Act of 2004. The argument, in this case, is that in the event a pregnant woman is subjected to a violent act and the unborn child is harmed or killed, the perpetrator of the act can be charged for the death or injury of the unborn child. On top of that, the perpetrator can be charged by the state even if the child was going to be aborted. This law changes the game a bit. The law makes it clear in the eyes of the law, the life of an unwanted child is not worth less than the life of a wanted child.

The last common line of reasoning for this argument is a non-secular approach based on Judeo-Christian values. In this case, the idea is that an abortion results in the destruction of a human life which amounts to murder, which is a breach in one of the ten commandments. This makes it a sin, an action which both religions try to avoid.

With what could be considered the main argument now discussed, numerous secondary arguments are used to counter specific points that are presented by the opposition. The counterargument to the argument that a woman has the right to decide what to do with her own body is that from the moment of conception, the unborn child has a unique sequence of DNA. As a result, a choice to harm the unborn child would be equivalent to harming any other human being. Another common argument is that abortion eliminates the potential contributions to society that the aborted children might have been able to make, had they been born and raised to adulthood. Yet another common argument against abortion is that abortion can occasionally lead to some medical problems and also cause psychological damage for the mother.

There is also an argument that abortion amounts to discrimination since it can be used to terminate genetically defective babies. The same argument has also been used regarding the African American community since the abortion rate is considerably higher in that demographic than in other groups.

The idea is that the higher abortion rate in their community is essentially a genocide against African American babies.

To cover a few more fringe arguments, it has also been suggested that it is unethical for a medical professional to perform an abortion. Since doctors typically have to take the Hippocratic oath before practicing medicine, they swear to do no harm, meaning that it would be a breach in this oath to take the life of an unborn child. Related to the value of human life, another argument is that abortions promote a cultural environment that strips human life of its value.

This loss of value could then lead to the acceptance of actions and crimes that are unthinkable currently, like euthanization of homeless or those that are deemed a burden to society. This is an extreme example, but history shows us that the extreme can occur with detrimental consequences. The last argument that appears somewhat frequently is one that places the responsibility of the pregnancy upon the woman. One line of reasoning related to this argument is that government money should not be spent providing abortions for women. The idea is that taxpayer money should not be used for abortions unless the majority of taxpayers support abortion. To do otherwise would be unethical.

Another argument placing responsibility with the woman is that if she consented to an unprotected sexual relationship, then she knew there was a risk of getting pregnant. She accepted that risk and the consequences that accompany it. The reasoning continues by asserting that an unborn child should not have to pay for the mistakes of others. An argument based on a combination of the two of these is that women should not be able to use abortion as a form of contraception since it would be immoral to kill an unborn child simply because it is convenient.

Once again, as a final remark and disclaimer, the arguments listed above do not represent all of the arguments in favor of pro-life. At an individual level many Republicans most likely only agree with a few of the arguments listed above. Another critical thing to note is that many Republicans will change their stance on abortion in the case of incest or rape. Some will then say that an abortion can be justified under those circumstances whereas others feel like rapists should be punished to the fullest extent of the law but that a baby conceived in rape should still have a right to live.

Another particular case occurs when the pregnancy puts the life of the mother at risk. In this case, many Republicans agree that the loss of the life of the child to preserve the life of the mother is very unfortunate but acceptable in this situation only. With that, we can wrap up the stances of the parties and move on to where we can compromise.

The Common Ground on the Issue of Abortion

After looking at both sides of the issue and now knowing some of the relevant facts, we are situated in an excellent position to weigh both sides of the argument. We will aim to draw some conclusions on the abortion issue that the majority of us will hopefully be able to agree on. The first significant conclusion that we can reach is that both sides of the argument are not directly opposed to each other. The Left does not necessarily support abortions, so much as they support the right for women to have abortions. The Right is completely against abortions in nearly all cases, but they hold this view for the sake of the child, not to oppress women. This seems bad, but it is not the same as being for and against abortion. The second major conclusion that can be drawn is that even though both sides are not directly in opposition on abortion, they feel very strongly about the issue so finding a compromise will be difficult because of the strength of the feelings that are felt on both sides.

The Left believes that abortions are a fundamental right for women, whereas the Right believes that abortions amount to the murder of unborn children. To further expand on the opinion of the Right, many feel that use of abortion in this nation essentially amounts to genocide, since in their eyes, more (future) American lives are lost to abortions every year than were lost during the entire civil war. To expand on the opinion of the Left, without abortion, millions of women would have had their lives torn apart to accommodate the birth of a child. To remove a woman's option to have an abortion would have the effect of forcing her into a complicated situation that could lead to acts of desperation.

Looking at the situation in this light, when one side views abortion as a right and the other side views it as an act of genocide, it does not seem like any compromise will be made on the issue beyond the compromises that are already in place. Fortunately for us, this is not the case, as there always exists some common ground.

In the case of abortion, the answer lies in taking action before it becomes a problem. This is not a new idea, but it is the most effective option that is available and one of the only options in which all sides win. Legislation that all parties can agree upon should be focused on minimizing the number of abortions. This is a win for the Right because their supporters will most likely support an effort to reduce abortions. This is also a win for the Left since they are not fans of abortions but still wish to maintain a degree of freedom for women to be able to make a choice to have an abortion if they decide it is the best course of action.

The means at our disposal to minimize the number of abortions lie in the use of proper education and contraceptives. Touching on contraceptives first, the use of contraceptives is always a good choice in intimate relationships where an unplanned pregnancy is not the desired outcome. Each form of contraceptive has its own degree of effectiveness, so first and foremost, abstinence is the best way to completely eliminate the risk of pregnancy and the risk of needing an abortion. This is simply because it is 100% effective by its very nature since no sex equals no pregnancy in nearly every single situation.

Abstinence aside, the Planned Parenthood website has information on other birth control methods that range in effectiveness from 71% to 99% [9]. Many of these birth control methods do not prevent the transmission of STDs and should not be used alone. Therefore, legislation that meets the needs of both sides of the argument should be focused on ensuring that any funding that is going towards Planned Parenthood or any other abortion-providing organization is funding for contraceptives. The intended aim is to ensure that contraceptives are available at a reasonable price and in the right geographical locations. This sort of legislation would have the highest chance of passing in our current divided political environment.

This sort of compromise is about the best that can be expected regarding funding related to abortion. The Right has no desire to fund abortions, but they may be willing to concede financing for programs that are focused on preventing the need for abortions. It is likely that many on the Right feel that it is not the government's responsibility to provide any funding towards contraceptives. Just as they think that abortions should not receive government funding. To the same point, it is also likely that many on the Left may feel that providing funding for contraceptives alone is not doing enough to address the issue at hand.

In reality, the best solution would probably be for individuals to take responsibility for their own reproduction related choices, as they are better equipped to determine what is best for each of their own situations. Barring this, a program that promotes the use of contraceptives is a benefit to our country since it would reduce the resources that need to be devoted to caring for children who would otherwise be aborted if they were conceived. Overall, this prevents the genocide the Right is opposed to and deals with the problem of unplanned pregnancy motivating the Left.

Contraceptives aside, education is the other effective method we have at our disposal to minimize the number of abortions. Abstinence-only based sex education programs make up the majority of sex education provided in American schools. Although abstinence provides several mental, emotional, and spiritual benefits and is completely effective when properly implemented, many individuals still choose to engage in sexual activity for various reasons. Since abstinence is the primary focus of sexual education, many individuals engaging in sexual activity are not adequately educated on the mechanics of human reproduction or the correct use of contraceptives. Statistics from 2010 indicate that only 70% of teen women and 62% of teen men received education on how to properly use other contraception methods [10]. These percentages are far too low for the number of teens who choose to engage in sexual activity.

Typically, the Right does not support individuals engaging in premarital sex. This would be a large part of the reason why most sexual education courses provided in schools are based on abstinence. Limiting schools to abstinence-only education is no longer practical if we, as a society, are hoping to limit the number of abortions that take place. In this case, the Right would have to compromise and be willing to allow schools to teach sex education that provides medically accurate information as well as information on how to implement other forms of contraception. The argument to counter potential pushback on the Right would be that more education is always better for society. Educating teens to prevent unplanned pregnancy would result in more individuals who can positively contribute to society without having to make tough choices regarding the life of an unborn child. Since a sizable component of the Left does not experience the same inhibition regarding premarital sex, they would hopefully readily agree to any programs that promote better sex education to reduce the number of abortions that occur.

Although both of these options to minimize the number of abortions are not necessarily ideal for either party, both represent legislation that is beneficial while also being potentially passable through a divided Congress. Whether or not any legislation based on these two compromises would pass through Congress would ultimately depend on the willingness of the serving representatives to work together for the sake of the American people.

As a final disclaimer, more compromises other than the two listed may also exist, once again this is not a conclusive or definitive discussion on the abortion issue. This chapter was intended to provide an overview of some of the facts, the relevant arguments, and provide a few compromises that meet some of the demands of each side. More than anything, we could make a large amount of progress if we could just accomplish one thing. If we could persuade Americans in the 15-30 age range that it is a risky idea to have sex before you are married and an utterly horrible idea to have unprotected sex, we could probably cut the abortion rate down considerably.

Second Edition Commentary:

Since writing this chapter in 2018, the abortion issue has changed substantially in the United States. On June 24, 2022, Roe v Wade was overturned during the ruling of the Dobbs v. Jackson Woman's Health Organization case. This effectively removed the "constitutional right to abortion" that existed prior to the ruling.

The fallout from this ruling was substantial. An argument could be made that it cost the Republican party the 2022 midterm elections. However, it's my opinion that the whole situation was blown vastly out of proportion. The overturn of Roe v Wade simply relegated abortion back to being a state issue instead of a federal issue. This seems like a better way to handle the issue of abortion because it allows a smaller group of people the ability to set the rules they must live by instead of having the Federal Government cramming the issue down from above.

Beyond that major change, the issue as whole is still basically the same. The Left still seems to be interested in unlimited abortion access. The Right wants nothing to do with it. The common ground compromise still remains the same. To solve the abortion issue, minimize the number of pregnancies that occur outside of wedlock.

Chapter 3: The Issue of Climate Change

Background:

Having now closed our dialogue on our first issue, we can move into the next one which happens to be climate change. We will start with some definitions. First and foremost, the term climate is defined as being how the atmosphere behaves over a long period. Weather, on the other hand, is defined as being how the atmosphere is behaving over a short period [11]. The climate for a given region is the average of the weather over a long period for that region. Recalling middle school Earth Science, the Earth has a variety of different climate zones that are based on temperature and precipitation. There are five primary climate zones that can be subdivided into additional zones. The five main climate zones are polar, cold mid-latitude, mild mid-latitude, dry, and tropical. With these definitions out of the way, we can get into the heart of the matter.

What follows will be a substantial oversimplification, but the Earth is more or less an isolated system that is in balance. Therefore, the energy it receives has to be equal to the energy it emits with the exception of the energy that it accumulates over time. This energy accumulation is most likely behind climate change. Fundamentally, the occurrence of a change in temperature requires energy input. Therefore, at a basic level, the processes that cause climate change at the scale of the whole planet have to be related to energy input to the planet as well. Since the Earth is isolated, any changes in energy have to come from the Sun, the Earth itself, or some outside source. Without a shift in energy flow or energy accumulation, the system should remain in balance, and the climate should remain stable as well.

Although the Earth is generally in a state of energy balance, that balance can shift over time. The Earth naturally experiences a certain degree of climate variation as a result of the energy input and output of the planet fluctuating over time. The exact cause of the natural variation is attributed to several sources such as receiving different amounts of energy from the Sun, natural increases in greenhouse gases, or increases in the amount of snow and ice present on the surface of the planet.

We will now go into detail on each of these sources of variation. Like most stars of its class, the Sun undergoes a solar cycle that results in the energy output of the Sun varying periodically between a maximum and a minimum amount. In the case of the Sun, the energy output varies on a roughly 11-year cycle. The energy output of each cycle as a whole differs as well with some cycles outputting higher levels of solar energy than others. This variation in solar energy over different time frames is theorized to have some effect on the climate and weather experienced on Earth [12]. Operating with the assumption that the Earth is an isolated system, the Sun is most likely the greatest influencer on the energy input to the Earth.

Although the energy input from the Sun is the most significant influence, other parts of the Earth system can have a substantial effect as well. In the same way that the amount of energy the Earth receives plays an important role in weather patterns and climate, the amount of energy the Earth retains also can have an effect on weather and climate. Different gases present in the Earth's atmosphere retain energy and reflect energy at different rates and at different wavelengths. The gases that are particularly effective at retaining energy in the wavelengths that are given off by the Earth are referred to as greenhouse gases. The name is a reference to how the gases work in the same manner that a greenhouse does. Energy in the form of solar radiation is allowed in, but not all of the energy is allowed to escape. As a result, the interior of the greenhouse ends up becoming warmer than the surrounding environment. The result is the same when it is applied to the Earth, with radiation that would usually be reflected back into space being captured by the greenhouse gases.

The idea is that higher concentrations of these greenhouse gases in the atmosphere result in a larger amount of energy being retained in the form of infrared radiation from the Sun. Some common greenhouse gases are carbon dioxide, chlorofluorocarbons (CFCs), hydrofluorocarbons (HCFCs or HFCs), methane, nitrous oxide, ozone, and then water vapor. Natural processes such as volcanic eruptions can release carbon dioxide and water vapor along with other greenhouse gases. This gas release can have an impact on regional and global climate depending on the scale of the eruption. With that said, we have discussed the energy input and energy accumulation of our Earth system.

The last major factor that can affect the Earth's energy balance would be the amount of energy that the planet emits back into space. As with the gases in the atmosphere, materials that make up the surface of the Earth absorb and emit solar radiation at different rates. Snow and ice happen to be very useful reflectors of solar radiation. This means that the amount of solar energy reflected back into space increases with the amount of the Earth's surface that is covered with ice and snow. Historical records indicate that the Earth has gone through several ice ages in the past where the amount of snow and ice on the surface of the Earth drastically increased. Likewise, there have been periods of warming during which the amount of ice decreased. These fluctuations have resulted in changes in the regional and global climate of the Earth in the past. All three of these processes together likely play a role in any climate change we are experiencing.

Where politics are concerned, the debate surrounding climate change usually centers around the climate variation caused by human activities and not on the naturally occurring variation in the Earth's climate. As a species, humankind currently cannot cost-effectively regulate the amount of solar radiation the Earth receives or the percentage of the Earth's surface that is covered by snow and ice. The same cannot be said about our effect on atmospheric composition. Ever since the industrial revolution 200 years ago, we have seemingly managed to increase the concentration of greenhouse gases that are present in the atmosphere. Since the industrial revolution, the amount of carbon dioxide present in the atmosphere has increased from about 280 ppm to around 408 ppm, as reported during 2018 [13]. This increase in atmospheric carbon dioxide has been accompanied by an average global temperature increase of 1.8 degrees Fahrenheit [14].

The increase in temperature has also potentially contributed to a decrease of 13.2% per decade of surface area covered by polar ice [14]. NASA provides additional information that indicates that since 2003, the total mass of Antarctic ice has been decreasing at a rate of 127 Gigatons per year with a margin of plus or minus 39. The same NASA information indicates that the total Greenland ice mass has been decreasing by a rate of 286 Gigatons per year with a margin of plus or minus 21 [14]. This melted ice has resulted in a sea level rise rate of about 3.2 mm or about 1/8th of an inch a year. In different terms, this has amounted to about 200 mm or 7.87 inches total of sea level rise from the year 1870 to the year 2000 [14].

In 2014, carbon dioxide made up the most significant component of the United States' greenhouse gas emissions at about 80.87%. Carbon dioxide was followed by methane, nitrous oxide, and other assorted gases at 10.64%, 5.87%, and 2.62% respectively. Looking at carbon dioxide emissions, specifically, the production of electricity contributes about 30.48% of emissions. This is followed by transportation emissions at 26.52%, industrial emissions at 21.41%, agricultural emissions at 9.16%, emissions from commercial applications at 6.65% and lastly residential emissions at 5.77% [15]. Focusing on the largest component, which is power generation, according to 2016 numbers, high carbon emission sources such as coal, natural gas, and petroleum make up about 65% of electricity production in the United States. The remaining 35% is produced through the combined generation of nuclear and renewable power sources, which have much lower carbon emissions [16].

Some potential consequences could result from the increase in atmospheric greenhouse gas concentrations that we have been observing. To name a few, the increase in global temperatures could result in more energetic weather systems since weather systems are primarily powered by differences in pressure and temperature between regions. The rise in sea levels could eventually result in the flooding of low-level land as well as certain coastal cities that lack flood prevention mechanisms. The absorption of carbon dioxide by the oceans could lead to disruptions in marine ecosystems as a result of the oceans becoming more acidic. Increases in global temperature could also render some regions dangerous to live in for individuals who are more susceptible to heat strokes or dehydration. Overall, these possible outcomes are not very pleasant. That aside, having discussed definitions, the Earth energy system, greenhouse gases, U.S. emissions, and potential consequences, we are now ready to begin discussing the party stances on this issue.

The Stance on the Left: Climate Change is a Major Threat

The current Democratic Party platform on climate change is that climate change is a real and urgent threat to the U.S. economy, national security, and the health and futures of American children. The Democratic Party believes that Americans deserve the jobs and the security that will result from the U.S. being a clean energy superpower in the 21st century [17]. The Democratic Party believes that several U.S. states and cities are already experiencing the effects of climate change through rising sea levels, drought, wildfires, super storms, and flash floods. The

Democratic Party believes that we, as a nation, need to take immediate, ambitious action across our economy to cut carbon pollution and greenhouse gas emissions.

The Democratic Party is committed to abiding by the Paris Agreement and keeping global temperatures below the 2-degree Celsius (3.6-degree Fahrenheit) increase threshold. They are committed to reaching some clean energy targets such as a point where half of the U.S.'s electricity production is produced by clean energy sources as well as having a target number of solar panels installed across the nation. They believe that the tax code should reflect a commitment to clean energy and that fossil fuel subsidies and tax breaks should be eliminated. They think that greenhouse gases should be priced to reflect their negative impact on the environment. The Democratic Party also believes that climate change disproportionately affects low-income and minority communities, amounting to "environmental racism" [18].

Overall, the argument for the position on the Left is pretty simple and follows the general form of presenting factual proof, detailing the likely consequences, and then proposing a solution to address the problem. The factual proof portion consists of evidence in support of climate change, some of these facts are listed in the background section above. The likely consequences portion will then include describing what will happen if we do not take action to prevent climate change. This is usually a combination of the possible consequences of climate change, some of which are also listed in the background section above. The last portion of the usual argument involves proposing a solution that will alleviate the effects of climate change. Usually, this proposed solution involves using more clean energy, limiting carbon emissions to certain levels, taxing the emission of greenhouse gases, or enforcing more strict regulations on companies that are directly and indirectly responsible for the production of large volumes of greenhouse gases.

The motivation behind this stance is also pretty simple. Assuming that humans are the cause of observable climate change, then we are also the cause of potential damage to the Earth. Since Earth is the only planet we can currently inhabit, doing too much damage to the Earth could lead to the end of our species. It is generally accepted that it would be unfortunate if we all died off, so that is something that we would like to avoid if possible. Additional support lies in realizing that the harm we are potentially causing could also be having an impact on the animals and plants that inhabit the Earth with us.

If we in good faith make the assumption that the factual basis in support of climate change is correct, then it is easy to see why climate change can transform into such a divisive issue. Those who support taking action to alleviate climate change essentially end up feeling like they are trapped up against a brick wall of facts. If the other side refuses to believe or even consider the facts which the climate change advocates have based their views upon, then there is no common ground, and the advocates are left feeling defeated and frustrated.

This frustration is then usually expended by making temperaments worse and eliminating any chance of an open dialogue taking place. With that said, we have now discussed the majority view held by the Democratic Party. Fringe stances also exist, but we will avoid discussing those fringe stances in this case in favor of moving on to our discussion of the Republican Party stance.

The Stance on the Right: Climate Change is an Expensive Issue

The Republican Party does not have a specific part of their party platform devoted to "Climate Change" related content. Instead, they focus on America's natural resources, specifically agriculture, energy, and the environment. The absence of a party platform devoted to climate change provides some insight into the lack of party consensus on the issue. The Republican Party at an individual level has a wide distribution of views on climate change. Views that range from outright denying climate change to viewing it as one of the lesser national security threats that we are currently facing. Therefore, lacking a direct address to climate change, the portion of the Republican Party Platform that addresses American natural resources can be summarized as being against government regulation for fear of it negatively impacting the economy where agriculture and energy are concerned.

This does not mean that the Republican Party completely disregards any potential damage that could be resulting from human activities. They reaffirm the moral obligation of all men and women to be good stewards of the God-given natural resources and beauty of the country we reside in [19]. They firmly believe that environmental problems are best solved by providing incentives for ingenuity and through the development of new technologies. They believe that progress is not made when there are extensive regulations that stifle economic growth [19].

The argument used by those who are considered climate deniers usually involves trying to discredit the possible impact that humans could be having on the environment through our activities. Some of the variations of this argument can make sense, but they are not always factually based. Some popular examples include stating that the Earth is too large to be affected by human activities, or that all of the carbon that is stored in fossil fuels was at one point in the atmosphere anyway. A better argument that does have some factual basis is stating that the Earth is just experiencing natural climate variation. In this case, the climate variation part of the argument is at least scientifically verified through evidence of carbon cycles and warming/cooling cycles.

Another argument that is growing in popularity would be that since our national competitors are not taking climate change seriously, we cannot afford to take it seriously either. The reasoning here is that even if the U.S. were to cut back on our use of fossil fuels for the sake of the environment, other countries we are trying to compete with economically, such as China and India, will not make the same cuts to emissions. So, we would essentially be handicapping ourselves while the environment would continue to grow worse. This stance has some merit but is not entirely reasonable since it is an extreme measure and assumes that we have no other options.

Moving away from the climate change denying end of the spectrum, the argument for believing that climate change is real, but being opposed to excessive regulations is stronger. The idea here is that the government should not be involved with regulating American industries in general. They should also not be in the business of taxing emissions. These actions are thought to stifle economic growth and potentially result in the loss of American jobs. Specifically, the loss of jobs would be the result of fossil fuel related industries having to downsize. Some examples of this would be power plants closing or mines shutting down in response to regulations or emission taxes making their business operations unprofitable. The majority of U.S. industries rely heavily on energy produced directly by sources of emissions. Since businesses rarely allow the erosion of their profit margins, the increase in energy cost as a result of emission regulations or taxes will be passed on to the U.S. consumer. Therefore, any taxes or regulations on emissions could also have the effect of increasing the cost of using these sources of energy. This will reduce the amount of money that consumers have available to pump back into the economy.

Looking at the heart of the matter, the thought is that instead of regulating companies, the government would provide incentives for companies to develop environmentally friendly technologies that reduce emissions. These incentives would promote the use of these technologies and give companies that are environmentally friendly a competitive advantage. This would effectively drive other companies to adopt the same technologies.

Overall, it appears like the primary concern of the Republican Party is a financial one. Very few people in the party are opposed to policies that are green or environmentally friendly. It is most often only when these policies are accompanied by a substantial economic cost that they are met with resistance from the Republican Party. This stance is easy enough to understand. It is difficult to justify supporting policies that will cost voters in the present while not providing a clear reward in the future.

A clean and healthy environment seems like a clear reward, but at present many people do not experience the adverse effects of our fossil fuel usage, so it is difficult to connect the dots, especially when it will potentially cost some Americans their jobs. With that, we have discussed the bulk of the Republican side of things, so we can transition to the possible compromises between the two parties.

The Common Ground on the Issue of Climate Change

Similar to abortion, many people on the Left and the Right are not directly opposed when considering the issue of climate change. Speaking in general, the Right does not support climate change, but instead they either do not believe that climate change is an issue, or they do not think the answer to climate change lies in the use of taxes or regulations. In the same way, the Left is not opposed to economic growth or Americans prospering, they are just fearful that the impacts of climate change could cause severe problems for the nation and the world as a whole. Obviously, there still are those on either side of the issue who hold the fringe views that are directly opposed to one another, but for the purpose of this book, we are operating under the assumption that the people who fall into these two categories make up a small fraction of the total number of people in our nation.

Legislation that meets the needs of both the Left and the Right should be in favor of promoting clean energy produced here in the United States. It should also be focused on fostering the growth of U.S. technology that is environmentally friendly. Both sides should be able to agree that clean energy produced in the U.S. is a good thing. It is good for the environment, it creates jobs, and it enables the U.S. to strengthen its energy independence. The same can be said regarding the development of environmentally friendly technology. There are many avenues through which this type of legislation could travel.

One example would be providing additional government funding in the form of research grants to institutions and companies that are developing environmentally friendly technologies. Another example that is already in limited implementation would be providing an incentive for consumers to buy environmentally friendly consumer goods such as electric cars. However, this would not be as effective at reducing emissions as one might suspect. The majority of the electricity that would be used to charge these electric cars would be produced by fossil fuel power plants. They would generate more emissions to cover the increased load from additional electric vehicles. A solution that would address this problem would be providing power companies with an incentive to generate more of their energy from environmentally friendly sources.

Perhaps the best way to address the problem with power plant emissions while also ensuring the energy demands of the U.S. are being met would be to restructure the regulations that govern nuclear power and promote education about nuclear energy. This would be to improve public opinion about nuclear energy and ensure that the general public begins to understand how safe nuclear power actually is and how effective nuclear power plants are at producing energy with limited emissions. One final example that is also partially implemented would be providing tax incentives to companies, towns, and cities that have a certain amount of their energy supplied by environmentally friendly sources.

Once again, although none of these options are entirely ideal for either party, they encompass many of the common interests of both parties on this issue. These ideas should be able to be passed through a divided Congress. Realistically speaking, any legislation that is not overly regulatory, and that is profitable or cost-neutral while also being environmentally friendly should be passable. Legislation of this sort is exactly what meets the needs of both parties.

Politics aside for a moment, the beautiful thing (in a poetic sense) about the current climate change situation in the U.S. is that environmentally friendly forms of energy have already captured the eye of industry and the general population. Even if the government chose to take zero actions, the combined efforts of companies and cities across the nation would probably be enough to reach the level of impact needed to ensure that the effects of human activities on the environment are kept to a minimum.

More than anything, we as consumers probably wield the most power to bring about the changes required to prevent further damage to our climate. If we choose to only drive energy efficient cars, to save energy where we can, to recycle, to vote for environmentally friendly candidates at all levels of government and to only support environmentally sustainable companies and projects we could probably force more positive change than any legislative action would be able to. We will wrap up on that positive note and transition to our next issue, which happens to be education.

Second Edition Commentary:

The climate change issue is best described as a dumpster fire. The benefit of four years has only further proven that there was a very large amount of fear mongering going on. Although climate change remains an issue, it's certainly not the life changing catastrophe that it was touted to be.

The technology front remains the most hopeful avenue of addressing climate change. At the time of writing the second edition update, Small Modular Nuclear Reactors (SMRs) are rapidly growing in popularity. The reduced size of the reactors allows a degree of factory mass production that was formerly impossible in the nuclear energy industry. Building the same SMR design repeatedly also cuts down substantially on the regulatory burden that accompanies the construction of traditional nuclear energy plants.

Overall, the common ground on climate change remains largely unchanged when compared to the first edition. Both sides still agree on sustainable technology being a good idea. Consumers seem to be on board and consequently our society seems to be headed in the correct direction given the true severity of the situation.

Chapter 4: The Issue of Education

Background:

Education is one of the most important aspects of life. Nothing else has as much influence on an individual. We usually have to spend a minimum of 12 years in school. In some cases, for specific career paths that number can jump up to 20 years of school. Education is also a facet of life that our government has a large amount of control over. From a political standpoint, education is a diverse issue, with many challenges that need to be addressed. For our purposes, we are going to focus on what are perhaps two of the most prominent education issues currently facing our nation. Those issues are the issue of school choice and the cost of attending college.

Starting with the issue of school choice, school choice is a process in which a school district grants parents the ability to choose what school their children are going to attend. Generally, public education is set up in such a way where each student is allocated a sum of taxpayer money. The school a student chooses to attend receives the funds set aside for providing an education to that particular student. Students typically have to attend a school in their school district, which is based on where they live. In the current system, schools then receive their funding based upon their enrollment numbers. In school choice, if the parents select another public school aside from the one that their child would usually attend based upon location, this new school would then receive additional funding when they get to count that new child in their enrollment total.

This part of the issue, in and of itself, is not a significant source of controversy and would be a non-issue if all students were limited to only attending public schools. The catch is that students can also attend charter schools and private schools. Typically, when parents choose to enroll their children in private schools, the parents are required to cover the cost of tuition. When school choice is implemented, parents wishing to have their children attend a private school receive a set amount of money from the school district that they live in to put towards the cost of tuition at a charter or private school. This sum of money is usually referred to as a voucher. A voucher is valued at less than the amount of money that a public school would receive if the child were enrolled there, but it is still a substantial sum of money when compared to getting nothing. Vouchers allow parents to have their children attend private or charter schools without having to pay the full cost of the tuition by themselves. This can be a significant help to many parents. In some cases, a voucher can be the deciding factor for families who would fall short of being able to finically support the cost of a private school.

A large number of students could potentially be affected by school choice. Currently, there are about 50.7 million students who are enrolled in public elementary and secondary schools [20]. This breaks down to about 35.6 million students in pre-kindergarten to the 8th-grade and about 15.1 million in the 9th to the 12th-grade [20]. In addition to this, there are around 5.2 million students who are expected to be enrolled in private elementary and secondary schools [20]. In 2014-2015 there were approximately 13,600 public school districts with about 98,200 public schools in the United States [20]. There were also around 6,700 charter schools and 34,600 private schools [20]. The expenditure on public schools during 2017-2018 was projected to be approximately $623.5 billion with per-student spending of $12,300 [20]. And with that, those statistics round out our background on school choice.

Moving on to the background surrounding the cost of college tuition, the issue here is pretty straightforward. Some level of a college education is expected to be required for 65% of all jobs the U.S. economy will need by the year 2020 [21]. As a result, to find gainful employment, attending college is almost all but required for students graduating high school. Additionally, many of the jobs requiring a college education are among the highest paying and most sought-after jobs. In terms of career selection, this provides an even greater incentive to attend college. As of 2015, 69.2% of high school graduates were immediately enrolled in college following their graduation [20]. In the fall of 2017, it is estimated that 20.4 million students were enrolled in U.S. colleges and universities [20]. Of these students, 7 million were attending 2-year colleges, and 13.4 million were attending 4-year colleges [20]. Once again, out of the 20.4 million, around 17.5 million students were expected to be enrolled in undergraduate programs with the remaining 3 million students being enrolled in graduate programs [20].

For the 2015-2016 academic year, the average total annual cost to a single student across all institutions for college tuition, fees, room, and housing was about $22,432 [22]. Twenty years earlier for the 1995-1996 academic year, this number was about $13,572 in 2015-2016 dollars [22]. Jumping back another twenty years further, the same figure was about $9,037 for the 1975-1976 academic year in 2015-2016 dollars [22]. Using the 2015-2016 number, 2 years of college would cost an individual about $44,864, 4 years of college would cost around $89,728, and an 8-year degree would cost approximately $179,456.

In 2013 the federal government spent $76 billion on higher education while state governments spent about $73 billion [23]. Only a component of this funding goes towards offsetting the cost of tuition for students attending college. On average, in 2013, the federal government paid around $2,100 per full-time equivalent student in Pell Grant funding. This funding does go directly to assisting with tuition costs [23]. The funds not given directly to students are spent providing federal student loans, supporting grants, and providing direct funding to universities. Lastly, it is purported that the college completion rate has been hovering around 50%. This means that only half of those enrolled in college will actually have a degree to show for it.

Both of these issues are a significant point of contention among Americans. This makes sense of course since nearly every American ends up experiencing the cost of college first hand or by paying for someone else to experience it. Additionally, almost every American ends up with children in a school system somewhere at some point in time. For this reason, these issues are essential to both the Democratic and Republican parties.

The Stance on the Left: Against School Choice/ For Increased Higher Education Funding

Starting with the Democratic Party first, in general, the Democratic Party is against allowing school choice and in support of increasing the amount of government funding provided for higher education [24]. The Democratic Party supports the expansion of nontraditional school options but is opposed to vouchers being used to divert funding away from public schools [24]. The general line of reasoning in support of this stance is that the funds diverted from public schools through the voucher system result in a reduced quality of education for students who are not able to transfer out of the public school system. Students of higher socioeconomic standing can afford the indirect costs in addition to the tuition costs that result from relocating to a different school. Students from families of lower socioeconomic status are unable to cover these costs. Some examples of these added costs include transportation, housing, and even food in some cases. Although school choice could potentially affect a higher number of people, college tuition is usually the education topic that receives more attention.

The Democratic Party is in support of increased investment in Pell Grants and providing more tax credits for higher education [24]. The reasoning in support of this position is that a strong educational foundation is an essential key to expanding opportunities for young adults [24]. Additionally, the Democratic Party supports the push to make community colleges free and continue to provide debt relief to college graduates [25]. The idea is that the reduced cost of education will result in more people being able to afford the costs of attending college. These highly educated individuals will then be able to make more exceptional contributions to society and go further in life. Therefore, an increase in education spending is ultimately equivalent to investing in America's future. From there additional supporting points are often made. It is often argued that people with college educations make better choices, make more money, spend more money, have lower crime rates, and are better for the economy. All of these points are reasonable to some degree, so it is easy to understand the supporting reasoning for this argument.

This is perhaps the most well-reasoned argument in favor of providing additional funding for college. Less well-reasoned arguments rely more on the emotional appeal of providing a direct personal benefit to the target audience. More scholarships and potentially free college sounds like an outstanding deal to younger people who are headed to college and to the parents of those younger people. Since these groups make up a sizable component of the population, it is easy to garner a lot of support without using much reason. With these two arguments covered, we have discussed two of the more common reasons people support additional college funding. We can now take a look at the Republican side of this issue.

The Stance on the Right: For School Choice/Against Increased Higher Education Funding

Jumping right in, the Republican Party supports the ability for parents to choose the school their children attend. The Republican Party is also against additional funding for higher education [26]. The Republican Party supports school choice because school choice offers an escape route to students trapped in failing schools. Students can leave schools that are struggling and attend schools that have higher graduation rates. Additionally, school choice also provides parents with more control over their children's education.

The argument in support of school choice is pretty straightforward. Several different spins can be applied to it, but fundamentally it comes down to parents wanting what is best for their own children. The reasoning is pretty simple. Although it would be preferable for all children to have the best quality education possible, if a parent has to choose between sending their child to a lower quality school and sending their child to a better school that they can afford, then the parent will most likely want what is in the best interest for their child. The voucher makes it possible for the parent to then reap the benefits of the taxes that they are already contributing to the education system since the voucher offsets the cost of sending their child to a higher priced private school in place of the public school their share of taxes would have gone to.

Aside from this argument, there is also a strong line of reasoning that would support the idea that parents have a fundamental right to decide where their children attend school. This argument is often brought up when school choice is discussed, but it misses the central point of the issue. Very few people disagree with parents having the right to choose what school their children attend. People do, however, disagree with taxpayer dollars being diverted away from public schools to fund the choices of parents who want to send their children to different schools. With all that said, we can move on to the Republican view on college funding.

The Republican Party is against increased federal higher education funding in the form of federal student aid [26]. The reasoning behind this stance is that the availability of federal student loans has allowed higher education institutions to inflate the cost of tuition. If these funds were not available, higher education institutions would be forced to provide their services at a more competitive price. On top of this concern, there is also the issue of the cost to taxpayers that additional college funding would result in. Additionally, the Republican Party is against any regulations that drive the cost of education higher.

There are several arguments against increasing federal college funding, but for the most part, they all are more or less centered on the cost. In the case of public high schools, taxpayers receive a consistent return on their money. Nearly everyone can agree that providing education up to the high school level for all people creates a major benefit for our society as a whole. This changes, however, when we reach the college level. Unlike in high school where students are required to learn a specific curriculum across the board, college students can decide what classes they enroll in.

This difference shifts the net benefit away from society as a whole to the individual receiving the educational funds. One student may choose to use taxpayer funding to diligently pursue a challenging and time-consuming medical degree. Another student may choose to use taxpayer funding to pursue a less challenging art history degree and spend all of his or her extra time relaxing. The lifetime career of the first student might result in some meaningful benefits to society, but the lifetime career contributions of the art history major might not significantly benefit society, especially if this student is unable to find a job.

In this case, one student is a good investment for taxpayers while the other is a much riskier investment. The fact that students can essentially spend taxpayer dollars without being held accountable to the taxpayer is one of the major sticking points on this issue. This is one of the reasons why it is easier to find support for providing loans. Loans have the effect of reducing the risk that society might not get a return on its investment in the life of a student. This risk is really what stands in the way of a free college education for everyone. If students could guarantee that they would be productive members of society, then free college would be easier to support.

Without a guarantee of a return on investment, the argument transforms into a debate about how college funding essentially amounts to wealth redistribution. Money is being taken from taxpayers and given to students without students being required to provide something in exchange. Once we reach this point, we have gotten to the heart of a different argument, which is the belief that a government should not be used to benefit specific groups of people over others. From this belief, it follows that it is unethical to tax citizens to give money to a select group of individuals. Doing so basically amounts to stealing, which is wrong. With that, we have more or less covered the Republican side of things, and we can now focus on making some compromises.

The Common Ground on the Issue of Education

In the case of the two issues addressed on the topic of education, both parties hold views that are almost complete opposites to each other. With that said, there are still a few possible compromises. The primary goal of both parties should be to look out for the best interests of the country as a whole. Since education is directly responsible for improving the quality of life for everyone living in the country, both parties should be interested in working together to improve the education system. So, at the very least, both the Republican and Democratic parties share a common motivation for positive action.

On the issue of school choice, one possible legislative solution would be to change the way that schools are funded. If we can improve the quality of education provided by public schools, parents would have no need to send their students elsewhere. Instead of the current system in which funds are allocated based on enrollment numbers, funds could instead be tied to student success rates. In this new system, all schools would receive a baseline level of funding, but additional funding beyond that would be distributed based on performance. Under a system like this, schools would be incentivized to ensure students are meeting academic requirements and that graduation rates are high. This would make public schools more competitive and increase the quality of education that public schools can provide. This is not a magic bullet solution though, as there are several drawbacks to such a system. One such drawback would be the tendency for the exploitation of the system. Wide is the gate and broad is the road that leads to destruction. Very often in life, the path of least resistance is chosen.

Instead of rising to the occasion, schools might potentially inflate performance metrics and graduation rates to receive higher funding. As a result, necessary countermeasures would need to be put in place to ensure that schools and students are earning the incentive funding fairly. One such way to do this would be to have a series of high school graduation exams similar to current college admission tests to verify that graduates have the necessary knowledge to succeed in their post-high school years. Another method would be tracking the vocational success of students at yearly intervals after they graduate high school.

Another drawback would be the potential for funding pitfalls to be created. Schools that are not up to the challenge of increasing their performance could potentially end up trapped in a state of receiving only the baseline funding level. This could possibly prevent such schools from having adequate funds to make the improvements required to increase performance, such as investing in better educational technology, programs, and teachers. In a case such as this, one possible solution would be to use the Department of Education to conduct an investigation to determine the root cause of the underperformance at the school in question. Once the investigation is completed, targeted actions could be taken to address the specific issue causing the underperformance problem.

Another general solution that both parties could potentially support would be drafting legislation that promotes online high school education. Online education is more cost effective when compared to traditional education, and it has widespread accessibility. As a result, a more compelling online education system could bridge the gap between low-income students trapped at underperforming schools and educational success. Students could work at their own pace anywhere they have access to an internet connection. They would essentially have complete control over their educational future.

The primary drawback to online education would be the decrease in social interactions that students would experience. If they do not go out of their way to maintain a group of friends, feelings of isolation and loneliness could occur. I should also mention that their social skills would probably suffer. As a result, measures to counteract this isolation would have to be taken. One such action could be something as simple as still requiring kids to gather at schools. They could continue to have classes together along with all of the usual socializing. They would just be learning at their own pace on a computer.

Another drawback could be psychological effects caused by online education itself. Since the technology is new and continually evolving, we have a limited understanding of its long-term impact and effectiveness. More research would probably need to be done before full implementation could occur. Whether we change our education funding system or promote more online education, either of these solutions could help us make forward progress on the issue of school choice.

Moving on to the issue of higher education funding, our two parties are pitted directly against each other in terms of approach. Certain factions of the Democratic Party are in support of fully paying for the undergraduate education of students whereas certain wings of the Republican Party are against any form of college tuition assistance being provided to students. With that said, there still exists a compromise that could allow each party to meet in the middle. That is, assuming these two parties truly support the advancement of Americans in higher education.

Such a compromise would be promoting legislation that lowers the cost of college across the board. The current problem with college tuition can be reduced to a question of economics. Since a large number of careers require a college education, the demand for a college education is exceedingly high. On the other hand, college degrees are difficult to obtain. This difficulty can be attributed to high tuition costs, admission requirements, and limited enrollment space for students.

This creates a situation in which the demand for a college education is higher than the supply, allowing colleges to charge high tuition without suffering a decrease in enrollment. From the principles of economics, the solution to such a problem would be to increase the availability of college. This would drive up the supply, and as a result, colleges would need to lower the cost of a college education to remain competitive. This would make college more affordable for students without costing taxpayers additional money in the form of financial aid on a year to year basis.

Therefore, legislation that increases the availability of college education should be legislation that is agreeable to both parties. Such legislation would include bills that ensure the regulations preventing the creation of new colleges are limited to only those required to protect the interests of students and the American people. Additionally, legislation that promotes the competition of existing colleges would also serve as a motivator to drive the cost down. Another possible alternative would be supporting and promoting legislation that expands the availability and accreditation of online higher education programs. Online higher education has the potential to increase the supply of higher education significantly and drastically drive the cost of college education down.

Again, using our economic model, the other way to address the college cost problem would be to lower the demand for college. This is more difficult than solving the supply side of the issue, but it is still feasible. In the workforce, a college degree is often treated as a certification of a person's ability to perform instead of a certification of a person's actual job-related knowledge. An employer can assume that a person who earned a college degree is capable of learning, responsible to some extent and somewhat intelligent. Anecdotal evidence indicates that many college graduates never use much of what they learned in college. Instead, upon landing a job, graduates are often trained by their new employer in the skills they will need to complete their job. So instead of using college as an expensive way to vet potential employees, legislative action could be taken to set up programs around the nation that provide certificates of competency.

These certificates would basically verify that potential employees have the necessary skills and a satisfactory ability to learn new things. The certificates would take a much shorter amount of time to earn than a college degree, but they would provide employers with the same assurance that the person they are hiring will be competent and capable of learning how to perform the intended job properly. A system like this would allow many students to forgo spending four years in a university in favor of starting their career right away. A college education would then only be needed by those professions that truly do require the degree and the variety of knowledge that colleges can provide. The shift of students getting certificates instead of attending college would then drop the demand for college and the cost as a result. This solution would require a substantial social change to be effectively implemented, so addressing college costs through the supply side would most likely be the best way to go.

Another potential solution to help the demand side of the college issue would be for high school graduates to simply wait a year or two before going to college. This is not the right path in all cases, but in situations where a graduate is unsure of what they want to major in, it can be a good idea to get a job and take some time for personal growth before enrolling in a college. With a completion rate of around 50%, college can be a costly mistake if a person does not successfully graduate. Even delayed graduation can cost thousands of dollars. It can be a significant advantage for an undecided graduate to take time to grow and mature before going to college. This time can help the graduate determine what they want to major in at college. The added maturity from time in the real world can also improve the likelihood of a person's college success. If more graduates took a pause before going to college, it would also further reduce demand for college, which would help lower the cost. Colleges would need to prove that college is worth attending. With that, we have covered a few compromises that could work for school choice and college tuition.

The solutions, as mentioned above, have the potential to meet the needs of American students while still aligning with the interests of both parties. Legislation that addresses these points should be passable even with a gridlocked legislative branch. This meets our goal of finding common ground between both ends of the spectrum, allowing us to move on to our next issue. One that will be much less fun in nature.

Second Edition Commentary:

Very little progress has been made on the education front in the last four years. For a brief period of time, it seemed like Covid might have a long-term impact on the college situation and education in general. I personally hoped that it would force a pivot toward personalized education plans for individual students.

That didn't prove to be the case. As restrictions were lifted, things not only returned to normal but also got worse. This is still hearsay at this point, but it appears like the students impacted by Covid will never make up for the educational progress they lost. This is unfortunate and it will likely have generational consequences. Only time will tell.

The price of college continues to rise year over year. There has been very little reform. During Covid, there was a pause on student loan payments. At the time of writing this, it looks like payments will resume shortly. Overall, the situation remains stagnant and the common ground improvements mentioned above remain valid.

Chapter 5: The Issue of Illicit Drug Use

Background:

With the issue of education behind us, another issue facing America is the issue of illicit drug use. Like usual, we will start with a few definitions. According to sciencedirect.com, illicit drugs are substances that stimulate or inhibit the central nervous system or cause hallucinogenic effects to a great enough degree that using these substances is globally prohibited. According to the same source, illicit drugs can also be classified by their major effects. The four main types are as follows: stimulants, depressants, narcotics, and hallucinogens. The following are some examples of each illicit drug type in their respective order: Cocaine, Xyrem (the date rape drug), Heroin and Lysergic Acid Diethylamide (LSD). Aside from these four, many other drugs are classified as being illicit. More information about specific drugs can be found on the DEA website www.dea.gov. With that, we have taken care of our definitions so we can now focus on more general facts related to illicit drugs.

In 2007 it was estimated that drug addiction and drug abuse cost the United States around $200 billion in healthcare costs, legal fees, criminal justice costs and lost workplace production/participation costs [27]. This amount of money is slightly less than the total 2017 GDP of Vermont, Wyoming, Montana, and South Dakota added together at around $220 billion [28]. According to the 2017 National Survey on Drug Use and Health (NSDUH), 30.5 million people or roughly 1 in 9 Americans age 12 or older, used an illicit drug in the last month [29]. Illicit drug use is even more common in younger Americans. The survey indicated that 1 out of 4 Americans aged 18 to 25 had used illicit drugs within the last month [29]. Marijuana is the primary illicit drug of choice. It is used by 26 million of the 30.5 million illicit drug users in America [29]. In second place following marijuana, 3.2 million Americans misused prescription drugs [29]. The remaining 1.3 million current illicit drug users were using at least one of a large group of drugs, such as cocaine, methamphetamines, hallucinogens, inhalants, heroin, prescription tranquilizers, stimulants or sedatives [29]. In our culture today, the two types of drugs that get the most attention are marijuana and opioids. We will focus on these two drugs in depth here.

The NSDUH allowed the estimation of opioid misuse in America. Opioid abuse is a combination of heroin use and prescription pain reliever misuse. According to the survey, around 11.4 million people misused opioids throughout 2017 [29]. 886,000 people misused heroin, about 562,000 people abused both heroin and prescription drugs, and 11.1 million people only misused prescription drugs [29]. The top reason for opioid misuse was to relieve pain at 62.6% [29]. Other reasons for use included: to feel good or to get high (13.2%), to relax or to relieve tension (8.4%), to help with sleep (5.4%), to help with feelings or emotions (3.6%), to experiment or see what it's like (2.8%), and lastly to use as a result of being hooked or having to have the drug (2.2%) [29]. The remaining 1.7% of users, used for some other reason or to alter the effects of other drugs [29].

53.1% of these drugs were acquired from a friend or relative in some way, 36.6% were obtained through a healthcare provider, 5.7% were obtained from a drug dealer or stranger, and 4.6% were gotten in some other way not listed in the survey [29]. In 2017, Hydrocodone was the most popular misused drug (6.26 million use cases), followed by Oxycodone (3.74 million), Codeine (2.83 million), Tramadol (1.75 million), Buprenorphine (766 thousand), Morphine (501 thousand), Methadone (261 thousand) and Fentanyl (245 thousand) [29]. In terms of age breakdown, 800 thousand opioid misusers were age 12 to 17, 2.5 million were age 18 to 25, and 8.1 million were age 26 or older [29]. That covers the usage information on opioids.

Turning our focus to marijuana, according to the NSDUH survey, around 26 million Americans older than 12 years of age were current users of marijuana in 2017 [29]. Over the same period, about 3 million people 12 years or older had tried marijuana for the first time, making it the fastest-growing illicit drug for that year [29]. About 26.1% of people surveyed in 2017 felt there was a considerable risk of harm from smoking marijuana once a month [29]. This number went up to 31.9% for the perceived risk of smoking marijuana once or twice a week [29]. In general, marijuana is considered to be the least dangerous substance to use when compared with cocaine, heroin, alcohol, and cigarettes [29].

On the topic of risk, the general population thinks that occasional drug use is a low to moderate risk. The real concern is the potential likelihood of drug use leading to substance dependency or addiction. The NSDUH used DSM-IV criteria for dependence or abuse to determine the number of people who suffered from possible substance addiction [29]. The criteria are as follows [29]:

- Spending a lot of time engaging in activities related to the use of a drug.
- Using a drug in greater quantities for a longer period of time than intended.
- Developing a tolerance to a drug.
- Making unsuccessful attempts on cutting down on the use of a drug.
- Continuing to use the drug despite physical health or emotional problems associated with use.
- Reducing or eliminating participation in other activities because of the use of a drug.
- Experiencing withdrawal symptoms when cutting back or stopping the use of a drug.

According to the above criteria, about 7.5 million people older than the age of 12 had at least one illicit drug use disorder during 2017 [29]. This number breaks down to about 741,000 people between the ages of 12 and 17, 2.5 million between the age of 18 and 25, and 4.3 million adults over the age of 26 [29]. These numbers are small relative to the total population of the country; however, they still represent a large number of people who are suffering as a result of drug use.

Related to illicit drug use, 20% of incarcerated people are locked up as a result of a drug offense [30]. That breaks down to about 456,000 people [30]. There are 6 times as many arrests for drug possession, as there are for drug sales [30]. Using the average national cost per inmate per year of $33,274, and the number above, these 456,000 people cost taxpayers around $15.172 billion a year [31]. There are more facets to this issue that could be discussed, but for an overview, the points we have covered above should be substantial to develop a general understanding of the issue.

The Stance on the Left: Prevention through Education and Treatment

According to the 2016 Democratic Party platform, the Democratic Party believes that we, as a nation, need to confront the epidemic of drug and alcohol addiction, specifically the opioid crisis [25]. They believe this should be done by expanding access to prevention and treatment, supporting recovery, helping community organizations, and promoting better practices by prescribers of drugs [25]. The Democratic Party will continue to fight to expand access to addiction treatment services and to ensure that insurance coverage for drug-related issues is equal to that for other health conditions [25]. They think it would be a good idea to do more to educate American youth, as well as their families, teachers, coaches, mentors, and friends about the risks of drug use [25].

The Democratic Party stance on this issue is straightforward to understand, and it requires little explanation. They prefer to view drug use as a medical issue as opposed to viewing it as a criminal activity. This perspective results in taking a different approach to addressing the issue. When drug use is considered to be a medical condition, more focus is placed on taking action to treat the condition instead of taking action to deal with the crime of individuals using the drugs. The best way to empathize with this view is to imagine that a family member has a problem with their weight. It makes more sense to help them develop healthier eating habits than to spend time trying to eliminate all of the unhealthy foods they might be able to access. With this said, we can move on to the Republican stance for this issue.

The Stance on the Right: Prevention through Legislative Action

According to the 2016 Republican Party platform, the Republican Party acknowledges that a drug problem does exist but does not outline a clear future action plan to address it [32]. Instead, the platform discusses some aspects of the drug issue and then points to the Comprehensive Addiction and Recovery Act (CARA) as being the solution to address the opioid epidemic from both the supply and demand side of the problem [32]. Like most legislation, CARA is long and wordy. However, in summary, CARA creates grants to address local drug crises and expands programs to buy back prescription drugs. It is entirely directed at dealing with the opioid crisis and does not address any other problems related to drug abuse.

Given the lack of information on the issue present in the party platform, there is little that needs to be explained to understand the Republican Party perspective. They view the drug problem as being a criminal problem that is either already being addressed or a low priority issue. Since that is the case, we will transition straight into discussing improvements that we can make to the current situation.

The Common Ground on Drug Abuse

Compared to many of the issues facing America today, the drug crisis is one of the issues that most Americans can agree on to some degree or another. In general, nearly all Americans would agree that incorrectly using drugs is not healthy for the human body. Additionally, most, if not all Americans would also agree that becoming dependent on a drug is not a good thing. This provides us with a large amount of common ground to work with, especially when compared to some of the other issues we have discussed.

Generally speaking, as individuals become more educated on the risks associated with a particular activity, they are less likely to participate in that activity. This leads to the first category of passable legislation that both parties could agree on to help deal with America's drug problem. Legislation that promotes the education of students and the general public on the risks associated with drug use should be able to find support with both parties. The Democrats already state in their party platform that they will support education targeted at drug prevention. Since addressing the drug problem would enhance the future of millions of Americans and make the country a better place to live in, the Republican Party will no doubt support additional drug awareness education as well since making America great is a big part of their party platform.

Another category of legislation that both parties could potentially agree upon would be legislation that provides more readily available access to emergency services for those suffering from drug overdoses. As it currently stands, when suffering from a drug overdose, many individuals do not seek medical attention until it is too late. This delay in seeking help is a result of the fear of facing legal consequences for being caught using illicit drugs. To many, especially when in an impaired state of mind, it seems like a better idea to ride things out than to risk going to jail or facing the consequences for drug use. Therefore, legislation that would reduce or eliminate legal consequences for those who seek medical assistance for a drug overdose would result in less overdose-related deaths. Some states already have laws in place that are like this or that are aimed at alcohol use only. Expanding these laws could save many lives.

A more radical way of addressing the drug problem would be legalizing all illicit drugs. This sounds like a horrible idea at first, but additional steps would be taken to make it work. For example, the next step after legalization would be allowing private companies to manufacture these newly legalized drugs and then using the FDA to regulate the quality, dosage, and distribution of these drugs in the same way prescription drugs are currently regulated. The final step would then be to levy appropriate taxes on the sale of these newly legalized drugs and use this tax money to fund public health in the same way the taxes from most tobacco products are currently used.

This idea could ultimately accomplish multiple goals single-handedly. First and foremost, legalizing illicit drugs would have the effect of removing the adrenaline rush that comes with defying authority. This adrenaline rush is a common reason why many individuals try drugs in the first place and then persistently continue to take drugs. Secondly, if these newly legalized drugs are sold for less than the amount of money drug dealers can make selling the illegal variety, organized drug crime will either have to lower their prices or be forced out of business. This could potentially eliminate a good deal of the drug-related crime in the nation. Thirdly, having the FDA regulate the quality and dosage of these drugs would most likely decrease the rate of overdoses and the likelihood of drug-related deaths while increasing the safety of using these drugs. Lastly, the companies selling these newly legalized drugs would no doubt create new jobs along with plenty of tax revenue. This, along with the revenue from the drug sales, would help the economy.

Unfortunately, what I just described is a long way away from realistic. This idea would likely have very little support from either party, but it would be the most direct way to address the problem. Education would also need to be included to address the risks of using these kinds of drugs along with the long-term consequences these drugs can have on the human body. Additionally, the same restrictions that are in place to prevent minors from using alcohol and tobacco would need to be implemented in this new system as well. So those are additional hurdles that would need to be dealt with.

Taking a step back, implementing any of these solutions could go a long way toward improving the current drug situation in America. Countless lives could be improved, so there exists a strong incentive for both parties to cooperate to address this issue. The parties aside, having now briefly discussed the background, the views of both parties along with some solutions to the drug issue, we can move on to one of the most divisive issues facing our nation.

Second Edition Commentary:

The drug situation in the United States has seen similar stagnation to the education situation. Since writing this in 2018, 10 additional states have legalized marijuana. That brings the total up to 27 states. As this has rolled out, we've seen little improvement in the situation as a whole.

I'm no longer convinced that legalizing all drugs is a good idea. I'd like to believe that people can be responsible for their own choices, but a lot of the data indicates that may not be the case. Instances of DUIs remain concerning.

I stand by the suggestion to promote education and provide resources to those suffering from drug related dependency. These two options remain within the realm of common ground compromise. Both sides still should be able to agree that both options have the potential to be helpful and effective and alleviating the problem despite their broader disagreements on the issue as a whole.

Chapter 6: The Issue of Gun Control

Background:

First things first, the terms gun, firearm, arm, and rifle all tend to be used interchangeably. In general, this is fine, and I will likewise use them interchangeably, but there are some slight differences between each term. Now let us start with a basic description of a gun. When simplified, a modern gun consists of a barrel, a trigger, a firing chamber, and a firing mechanism. A cartridge, which consists of a projectile, a casing, a primer, and an explosive is required to operate a gun. This cartridge is inserted into the firing chamber. The gun is fired when the trigger is pulled. This activates the firing mechanism. The firing mechanism strikes the primer at the back of the cartridge. The primer explodes which causes the explosive powder to explode as well.

This explosion propels the projectile along the barrel and out of the gun at a very high speed. Many modern guns also have a magazine which is a container that allows the storage of additional cartridges. These cartridges are also referred to as ammunition. Googling "how guns work" and watching some of the resulting videos is the best way to make sense of this description. This description included the fundamental components that make up a gun. However, these components can be modified to create different classes of guns that have different functions.

Generally speaking, we can use these different functional classes to categorize guns. The exact categories can be a bit subjective, but most often, guns are divided into handguns and long guns. Long guns can then be subdivided into rifles and shotguns. Each type of gun has a set of unique characteristics, but the lines between each can be blurred through design or modifications, as I mentioned earlier. Handguns are generally small enough weapons to be fired by hand without having to brace the gun with one's body. According to 26 U.S.C 5845(a)(4), a handgun would be a weapon with an overall length less than 26 inches or a barrel length less than 16 inches. Handguns are easily concealed and generally only accurate at shorter ranges. Long guns, as one might have guessed, are weapons that exceed the length requirement of handguns.

Long guns that have rifling present on the inside of the gun barrel are generally classified as rifles. This rifling consists of spiraled grooves that run the inside length of the gun barrel. The addition of rifling causes bullets to spiral as they pass through the barrel. This spiraling provides additional stability and increases the effective range and accuracy of bullets fired from a rifle. Rifles have a much longer effective range and much better accuracy when compared to handguns.

Unlike rifles, shotguns do not generally have rifling cut into the inside of the gun barrel. Instead, the gun barrel of a shotgun is usually smooth. Shotguns typically fire a projectile that consists of a bunch of smaller BBs known as shot. This is different from a rifle which normally fires a single, solid projectile. Shotguns generally are a lot less accurate and have a shorter range than a rifle or handgun. In exchange for their lack of accuracy and range, shotguns tend to be more destructive.

Most guns fall into one of these three categories. However, certain guns have distinct features that might result in them not qualifying as a handgun, shotgun, or rifle. Handguns, shotguns, and rifles can be further classified based on the type of firing mechanisms installed on the respective gun. The firing mechanism is called the action. Guns can be manufactured with many different kinds of actions, but generally, they fall into three categories, which are single shot, semi-automatic, and fully automatic. A single shot firing gun requires the operator to manually reload the weapon between each pull of the trigger. A semi-automatic gun fires one shot each time the trigger is pulled and then automatically reloads the weapon between each trigger pull. This goes on until the weapon is out of ammunition. A fully automatic gun will fire a shot when the trigger is first pulled and then continue to fire and reload ammunition so long as the trigger is held down and ammunition remains in the magazine. The type of action also plays a role in determining how difficult it is to purchase a certain style of a firearm as a citizen.

The process to acquire a gun varies wildly depending on the location of purchase. In some states, a license or permit is required to own any firearm. Some states only require a license or permit to own a handgun. The majority of states do not require a specific permit but do require the individual purchasing the firearm to fill out a 4473 form and undergo a background check. If the person purchasing the firearm is not a prohibited person (a complete list of prohibited persons appears a few paragraphs below) and if they pass the mandatory background check, they will be able to purchase a firearm.

Once an individual has a gun, there are a few basic rules that can be followed to ensure proper safety. The five NRA gun safety rules are as follows:

- Always keep the gun pointed in a safe direction, whether loaded or unloaded and never point it at something you do not intend to shoot.
- Always keep your finger off of the trigger unless you are ready to shoot.
- Always keep the gun unloaded until you are ready to shoot.
- Always be aware of what is behind your target.
- Never use any alcohol or drugs that might impair your awareness or judgment when you are handling a firearm.

Following these rules will generally ensure that accidents or gun-related injuries are prevented. These rules make up a solid base for gun safety and are widely known by a large number of American citizens who own guns.

Once a gun is safely in hand, there are many gun laws in place that vary from state to state. These laws dictate when and where a gun can be carried. We will not discuss them in great depth because there is little consistency from state to state, but we will go over the basics. Some states have constitutional carry, in which an unloaded gun may be openly carried by citizens in some places. Most states will also allow citizens to acquire a permit to carry a loaded weapon concealed on their person. This is known as a concealed carry permit, a concealed weapon permit or a dangerous weapon permit. A citizen will have to pass a background check and often pass a training course of some sort. After accomplishing this, a citizen will then be awarded their permit.

With the concealed carry permit, a citizen can carry a weapon concealed in most public places, but there are a few exceptions. Although the list varies depending on the state, weapons cannot be carried concealed in schools, in airports or in government buildings. These permits are recognized in their issuing state for sure, but they can also be recognized in other states as well through a process known as reciprocity. States that have concealed weapon permit reciprocity with each other will let citizens from other states carry weapons in their state in exchange for other states returning the favor. With that said, some states refuse to honor this reciprocity. As a result, permit holders need to be aware of the local laws when they are traveling.

Taking a few steps back, the right for an American citizen to own a gun is derived from the Second Amendment to the United States Constitution. The Second Amendment states, "A well-regulated Militia, being necessary to the security of a free State, the right of the people to keep and bear Arms, shall not be infringed." As of 2014, there were around 371 million firearms in the U.S. owned by civilians and domestic law enforcement, with 39% of those firearms being handguns [33]. A 2016 survey indicated that somewhere between 36% and 49% of U.S.

households have a gun and that around 23% to 36% of U.S. adults own a gun [33]. This can be broken down further into 45% of males owning a gun compared to 15% of females [33]. 33% of white people own guns compared to 22% of non-white people [33]. 38% of Republicans, 31% of Independents and 22% of Democrats are reported to own guns [33]. 60% of people surveyed say they own a gun for protection from crime, 36% for hunting, and 21% for target shooting or recreational purposes [33]. In 2014 there were 586 fatal firearm accidents which made up about 0.4% of the roughly 136,053 fatal accidents for that year [33]. 148 of those 586 accidents occurred to individuals in the 15-24 age range [33]. In 2014 there were around 16,000 non-fatal firearm accidents which made up 0.06% of the 29 million accident related emergency room visits for that year [33].

Focusing on the topic of gun-related crimes, guns were used in 73% of the roughly 16,459 murders that were committed in the United States in 2016 [33]. Two years prior, in 2014, 5.9 million violent crimes were committed, 10% of which were committed by a criminal with a gun [33]. A study from the year 2000 estimated that U.S. citizens used guns for self-defense about 989,883 times per year [33]. A 1982 survey of felons indicated that 34% of felons had been scared off, shot at, wounded or captured by an armed victim [33]. 40% decided not to commit a crime because they thought a victim was armed [33]. 69% of the felons surveyed knew other criminals who had been scared off, shot at, wounded or captured by an armed victim [33]. 40% of the guns used in these crimes were acquired through an illegal street source [33]. 37.4% were acquired from family or friends, 7.3% were purchased at a retail store, 2.6% were purchased from a pawn shop, 0.8% were purchased through a gun show, and 0.6% were purchased at a flea market [33]. That covers the crime and where the weapons to commit the crime originated from. The next question would be what is being done to deal with this problem?

Currently, there are a substantial number of laws on the books that relate to or regulate guns. The laws that govern who can and who cannot have dealings with firearms are some of the most important gun laws currently under implementation. It is this class of law that we will focus on now. By law, it is illegal and punishable by up to 10 years in prison for any of the following people to receive, possess, or transport a firearm or ammunition: an individual convicted or under indictment for a felony punishable by more than one year in prison, an individual convicted of a misdemeanor punishable by more than 2 years in prison, a fugitive from justice, an unlawful user of any controlled substance, someone who has been ruled as mentally defective or has been committed to a mental institution, an illegal alien, a dishonorably discharged military member, someone who renounced his or her U.S. citizenship, someone subjected to certain restraining orders or someone convicted of a domestic violence misdemeanor [33].

On top of the ownership restrictions placed on the people in these groups, it is illegal for any federally licensed firearm business to sell or transfer any firearm without first conducting a background check to see if the buyer/recipient falls into one of the prohibited person categories [33]. The same law applies to private citizens as well. This is with the exception that private citizens do not have to perform a background check [33]. From 1998 to 2014, 202.5 million background checks were performed [33]. Of these 202.5 million background checks, about 1.2 million resulted in the purchaser being denied the right to purchase a firearm [33]. Beyond this general law, gun laws become much more nuanced on a state-by-state basis. Since this is the case, we will avoid getting into these smaller regional laws.

With the laws behind us, we will quickly look at a few trends. The sources I read through listed a few gun-related patterns that were of moderate interest. Generally speaking, handgun bans seem to result in an increase in murder rates to an eventual peak and then a decline over several decades. This trend can be observed with the cities of Chicago and Washington D.C. along with the countries of England and Wales. Right to carry laws, laws that permit all citizens to carry firearms, generally, appear to result in a decrease in murder rates. This can be seen in Florida, Michigan, and Texas [33]. These are general cases, though, and by no means a concrete rule. With these trends now stated, we can wrap up our background and begin looking at the party stances on gun control.

The Stance on the Left: Sensible Regulation

Starting with the Democrats and paraphrasing from the Democratic Party platform, the Democratic Party is in support of sensible gun regulation. They believe that we need to take sensible action to address gun violence. They propose that we do this by expanding background checks and closing loopholes that exist in our current gun laws. They would like to repeal the Protection of Lawful Commerce in Arms Act, which gives gun manufacturers legal immunity from lawsuits as a result of how their products are used. Additionally, they would like to keep "weapons of war" such as "assault weapons and large capacity ammunition magazines" off of the streets. They would like to provide the Center for Disease Control and Prevention with more funding to conduct more research on gun violence. Overall, the Democratic Party believes we should do more to keep guns from falling into the wrong hands. Some Democrats hold the fringe position that private gun ownership should be outright banned. This is an extreme position that most of the party does not openly support.

It is easy to understand why the Democratic Party supports expanding background checks and closing loopholes. We all can agree that we do not want criminals or high-risk individuals getting ahold of weapons. Avoiding background checks and exploiting loopholes are the primary aims of those individuals who would not be able to obtain a firearm legally. So, it makes logical sense to make it difficult to dodge background checks. From here, some of the stances the Democratic Party supports are more difficult to understand.

Repealing the Protection of Lawful Commerce in Arms Act would essentially force arms manufacturers to bear the legal liability for how their products are used. This would make it financially risky for arms manufacturers to produce products that could be used to cause a large amount of damage. As a result, arms manufacturers would have to limit their products to arms which have little potential for creating large amounts of damage. This could be done by designing guns to be slow firing or making them much more conspicuous and cumbersome. After all, it would be challenging to commit a crime with a 7-foot-long (2.13 meter-long), bright orange, 50-pound (22.7 kilograms) gun that only fires 1 shot every minute. This would probably have the effect of forcing arms manufacturers out of business since few people would want such a contraption.

That aside, removing "weapons of war" from the streets is also easy enough to understand. Having deadly weapons that are designed for life and death combat situations, in the streets, where irresponsible individuals can access them does seem dangerous. Soldiers go through weeks of training to learn how to operate some of these "weapons of war" effectively. So naturally, it seems like a good idea to only have these weapons available to properly trained and psychologically stable individuals. Also, to this point, it is often said that citizens have little need for combat grade weapons. Especially when we have a fully functional police force with combat grade weapons to provide protection for citizens. This position, at the very least, seems reasonable.

It is more difficult to say the same for the fringe stance. The concept of an outright gun ban is straightforward. The idea is that if no one has any guns, then it would be impossible to commit gun crimes. Moving past the concept, the idea of a gun ban is reasonable if it can be effectively implemented. If all guns were banned and taken off of the streets overnight, then going forward, any crimes committed would have to be carried out using knives or some other sort of weapon. This would be an improvement to our current situation, so it makes sense for a person to want this outcome. The prospect of being stabbed seems much better than the prospect of getting shot.

The question that remains is how one would go about implementing a complete gun ban that would successfully remove all guns from everyone. A proposal to pull that off usually is not discussed. Assuming that gun owners resist the confiscation of their guns, it would ultimately take more guns to ban guns than we probably have in the U.S. right now. As a result, a gun ban does not seem like a feat that could be easily accomplished. Since this fringe stance is not concerned with the actual implementation, but rather with the concept of a gun ban, we will wrap up here and transition into the Republican side of gun control.

The Stance on the Right: Against Additional Regulations

Jumping right in and paraphrasing from the Republican Party platform, the Republican Party firmly supports the Second Amendment right for individuals to own guns. As a result, they support constitutional carry, which would give all citizens the right to carry a firearm at all times. They also support reciprocity in all 50 states for law-abiding citizens who already have a permit to carry a gun in their home state. The Republican Party does not support any laws or regulations that restrict the capacity of magazines or ban common or modern rifles. They are against legislation that would enable lawsuits against gun manufacturers. Republicans are also against any laws that mandate the registration of any guns that are owned by law abiding citizens.

For our examination of these stances, let us start at the top and work our way down. Supporters of the Second Amendment right to keep and bear arms justify their support with many different lines of reasoning. Supporting the Second Amendment simply because it is part of the Constitution is reason enough for many. In addition to this, many people believe that the Second Amendment is the most important right Americans possess because it serves to protect and preserve all of the other rights listed in the Constitution.

The idea is that the government has a powerful obligation to serve the citizens of our country, faithfully. Unlike governments controlling unarmed citizens, the failure of our government to uphold this obligation could result in an armed revolt. If that were to happen, our unfaithful government would be overthrown and eliminated with the arms that the general population has possession of. Through this check, citizens can keep the government under control. After all, it is a great deal more difficult to take the freedom of speech away from a group of men with rifles than it is to take the same right away from a group of unarmed men. So, in essence, some who hold this stance hold it because the Second Amendment serves to keep government power in check.

Others who support the Second Amendment do so for their own protection. The Second Amendment can be viewed as a deterrent to crime. The common argument is that police response times are usually around 7 minutes or greater in most places in the nation. In some areas, the response time is much greater. In 7 minutes, a criminal could easily enter a person's home and harm the whole family before the police would be able to respond. Therefore, the right to own a firearm serves as a means of self-defense. Support of this stance, for this reason, should be really easy to understand, after all, who among us would not do anything it takes to keep our families safe. This desire to protect loved ones is a lot easier to empathize with than a desire to prevent government tyranny, which makes this a very compelling argument.

An additional reason some people support the Second Amendment is that some people just think that guns are cool in the same way some people think cars, sports or art exhibits are cool. They are fascinated with guns and want guns around for that reason alone. If you do not share this wonder and fascination, then it can be difficult to understand why someone would feel that way, but it is nevertheless reasonable.

The Second Amendment also provides the grounds for Republican support of constitutional carry. Since the right of the people to keep and bear arms shall not be infringed, it logically follows that people should be able to bear these arms without restriction. Beyond this, there are not many other lines of reasoning in support of constitutional carry. The argument for concealed carry permit reciprocity is a bit more reasonable. The idea is that a permit to carry a weapon should be valid in every state in the same way a driver's license is valid in every state. The reasoning in support of this is that the point of carrying a concealed weapon is to defend oneself and one's loved ones. This self-defense should not be sacrificed when traveling to or in a different state. This stance is even more reasonable if the travel destination is a higher risk area where self-defense might be needed.

The view against banning modern rifles and high-capacity magazines is also straightforward. The reasoning is that magazine size does not meaningfully limit the amount of damage a gun can cause in the wrong hands. It only takes a few seconds to reload a weapon, so limiting magazine size has a limited effect. Banning modern rifles and high-capacity magazines also has the potential to reduce the effectiveness of the citizen population at keeping the government in check. Both of these points make sense and are reasonable.

The belief that arms manufacturers should not be responsible for how their products are used is also rational. The idea is that it would be absurd to hold manufacturers liable for how their customers use their products. It would lead to many other companies being held legally responsible for how their products are used. Alcohol manufacturers could be held responsible for the behavior of people intoxicated from the use of their products. Car manufacturers could be held responsible for car crashes. Toaster manufacturers could be held responsible for bagel induced fires. The list of liability goes on endlessly and becomes much messier. With this being the case, it is easy to see why someone might not think holding gun manufacturers responsible is a good idea. It could open a can of legal worms.

The last Republican gun control stance we will look at is perhaps the most paranoid of the positions outlined in their platform. Unfortunately, it is still reasonable and valid to a certain degree. The most common reason Republicans do not support mandatory gun registration is that they fear that it would give the government the power to potentially discriminate against gun owners in the future. In a worst-case scenario, such a registration list could be used to systematically confiscate firearms from law abiding citizens. This could jeopardize the other freedoms we enjoy that guns protect. Essentially, the idea is that gun registration would give the government more power than the government can safely be trusted with.

With that said, we more or less can wrap up the Republican side of the gun control argument. There are a few stances that we did not discuss, but we did cover all of the major things that they mentioned in their party platform. So, with that taken care of, we can move on to looking at the compromises that can be made between the two sides.

The Common Ground on Gun Control

Although both parties are stringently opposed on the issue of gun control, like usual, there are a few compromises that both parties should be able to agree on. The first obvious compromise is the one that we have heard quite a few times over the years. Both parties should support the enforcement of the gun regulation laws that already exist. To that end, both parties should also support legislation that provides the necessary resources to law enforcement to ensure that our law enforcement officers can effectively prevent criminals and prohibited persons from being able to acquire firearms illegally. Both parties should also be willing to support legislation that enhances the tracking of mentally ill individuals since it is these individuals who pose the largest gun-related threat to other citizens.

In addition to agreeing on the enforcement of existing laws, both parties should be able to agree on passing legislation that invests in the development of better gun safety technology. Many of the firearms that criminals use to commit crimes are acquired through family members or from friends. If technology could be developed and implemented that would ID lock firearms to the owner, it would then be impossible for the firearms to be used by individuals who normally would be prohibited from possessing a firearm. To a determined criminal with substantial technical knowledge, this kind of protection would no doubt be defeated, since all systems can eventually be exploited and made to fail. However, to an individual who lacks such technical knowledge, such as a child or a less determined criminal, this sort of technology could be effective in preventing crime and potential accidents from occurring.

Another path of legislative action that both parties should be able to support would be promoting better gun safety education. Many U.S. citizens never receive formal firearm handling instruction. As a result of this, media sources such as video games and movies make up most of firearm usage training many citizens receive. As one might imagine, for the sake of action and excitement, both movies and videogames leave out important information on how to properly store and handle firearms. Therefore, legislation that would provide funding and a mandate for schools to teach students how to properly handle, store, and behave around firearms could potentially have many positive impacts. Students would no doubt take firearms more seriously. The knowledge of proper safety and storage procedures for firearms would also most likely result in fewer accidents. Storing firearms safely would also reduce the likelihood of them being stolen or misused.

The last commonsense compromise that seems obvious would be reducing the number of soft targets that are present in our towns and cities. The majority of mass shootings take place at locations that the shooter knows will not be heavily defended. Most commonly, these places include schools, churches, public events, and recreation areas. In the case of schools, improving security to address the problem has been suggested before. In many cases, this idea receives push back from individuals who do not want children to be exposed to a militarized environment that could result from increased security. With that said, there is still a lot that can be done to improve the protection that a given location has without having heavily armed officers marching up and down the halls.

Passing legislation that would require new schools to be built within a certain distance of a police station would be one possible action that could have meaningful benefits. Another possible action would be more frequent police patrols that pass near schools, theaters, public events, and churches when events are in session. In the case of schools, another potential course of action would be to pass legislation that provides funding for compartmentalizing schools with automatically activated bullet resistant doors and barriers. In the event of a shooting, the shooter could be remotely isolated in one section of the building away from as many people as possible. Realistically, having more school resource officers who are better trained and better armed also seems like a reasonable idea. After all, it is probably less traumatizing for a child to grow up around armed police officers than to witness a close friend or classmate being shot and potentially killed.

All and all, any of these suggestions has components that both parties should be able to support assuming that they truly have the best interest of our nation at heart like they claim to. Everyone should be able to get behind taking action that does not compromise gun rights while also protecting students and the general public from massive tragedies.

Second Edition Commentary:

The issue of gun control remains a major problem in the United States. Since 2018, there have been a number of pretty serious shootings. The cause for the majority of these incidents can be traced back to mental health issues. In general, mental health has been deteriorating since 2018 so the situation isn't improving on that front.

The growth of 3D printing technology and the advent of Ghost Guns has also acted as a bit of a game changer. The ability of civilians to manufacture working firearms has made it even less feasible to attempt a major crackdown on the number of firearms in circulation.

Nevertheless, the compromises suggested in the first edition of this book remain valid now. These mass shootings continue to target soft targets. Many of the perpetrators of the mass shootings have been shown to be in violation of existing gun laws. Gun safety still isn't widely taught in schools.

Teaching gun safety in schools, enforcing existing laws, and providing more security in high-risk areas all remain valid common ground solutions to the gun control issue.

Chapter 7: The Issue of Hate Speech

Background:

Having discussed gun control, we are now going to transition to an issue that is a bit more abstract. Hate speech is a tricky issue facing America. The First Amendment to the U.S. Constitution protects the freedom of speech, no matter how offensive the content of any given speech may be. However, the First Amendment does not protect the right to make threats, to harass someone, or to create a pervasively hostile environment. Currently, hate speech does not have a legal definition under U.S. law. There are, however, some general standards that are used when determining if a particular instance of speech qualifies as hate speech. Generally speaking, any expression that intends to vilify, humiliate, or incite hatred against a group or class of persons is classified as hate speech. As things currently stand, this type of speech can only be criminalized when it directly incites imminent criminal activity or contains threats of violence directed at a person or group [34].

Since freedom of speech is guaranteed in the Constitution, matters pertaining to freedom of speech are usually handled by the judicial branch of our government. As a result of this, several instances have resulted in legal precedents being established related to the freedom of speech. In the 1969 Brandenburg v. Ohio case, the Supreme Court ruled that the speech of a member of the Ku Klux Klan was protected as free speech even though it was hateful and disparaging towards African Americans. In 1978 the Supreme Court upheld a ruling in Collin v. Smith that allowed a group of neo-Nazis to march on the streets of an Illinois suburb where a large Jewish population lived. Boos v. Barry in 1988 resulted in a decision that stated we must tolerate insulting and even outrageous speech in order to provide adequate 'breathing space' to the freedoms protected by the First Amendment. In 1992,

R.A.V. v. The City of St. Paul saw the conviction overturned for a teen convicted of burning a cross on the lawn of an African American family. The act was considered to be protected by free speech. More recently, in 2011 the Supreme Court set aside a civil judgment that punished the Westboro Baptist Church for picketing a military funeral with disparaging signs that targeted the dead officer, LGBTQ persons, and the U.S. government in the Snyder v. Phelps case.

All these rulings indicate that there is a solid historical precedent for tolerating offensive speech for the sake of protecting free speech at large. This also wraps up the information we need to cover in our background on the freedom of speech debate.

The Stance on the Left: Regulate Hate Speech

Moving on to the Democratic side of the speech debate, according to their party platform, the Democratic Party wishes to promote civility. They speak out against bigotry and other forms of intolerance that have entered the political discourse of our nation. They feel that it is unacceptable to target, defame, or exclude anyone based on their race, ethnicity, national origin, language, religion, gender, age, or any other personal characteristic. They recognize that freedom of expression is a fundamental constitutional principle. But they believe that we must condemn hate speech everywhere it can be found. The Democratic Party condemns the current president's demonization of prisoners of war, women, Muslims, Mexicans, and people with disabilities along with his ties to white supremacists and the climate of bigotry he is creating. They also condemn the recent uptick in other forms of hate speech like antisemitism and Islamophobia. [25]

In this case, little explanation is needed to understand the Democratic views on this stance. We just need to take a look at human nature to understand where it stems from. Very few of us enjoy being insulted, degraded, or ridiculed. Usually being abused, degraded, or ridiculed results in the formation of animosity, resentment, and bitterness. Hate speech often incorporates these degrading elements and therefore, fosters the creation of the three negative responses I just mentioned. In general, we as individuals would rather avoid feeling this way.

We all desire to feel loved and accepted, not discriminated against. Therefore, if we can make people not say things that result in our feelings being hurt, it seems like a rational choice to do just that. This is what the Democratic party seemingly would like to do. They want to eliminate the possibility of being offended or discriminated against. I think their intended aim is to level the playing field for everyone involved. With that said, we can move on to discussing why the Republicans disagree with this line of reasoning.

The Stance on the Right: Protect All Speech

The 2016 Republican Party platform does not directly address hate speech. As a result, there is not much to say on the matter. I will, however, attempt to convey the view on this issue that I think many Republicans hold. From what I can gather, the Republican Party largely views hate speech as a non-issue. The Republican stance is that so long as any given exercise of speech does not result in violence or lead to immediate criminal activity, then it is protected by the First Amendment. They hold this stance because freedom of speech is one of the greatest safeguards of liberty. They believe that any infringement upon it carries considerable risk to society as a whole.

The reasoning behind this stance is that the limiting of speech is subjective. What one group may define as hate speech; another group may identify as the truth. With this being the case, there exists the potential for the group in power to define anything they find displeasing as hate speech. If hate speech is then outlawed, this group can effectively control the narrative and as a result, the people as a whole through the use of one-sided information. Many Republicans think this is actually what the Democrats are up to with the rise of intersectionality.

The Common Ground on the Issue of Hate Speech

This is one issue facing America where the best solution to the problem is not really a legislative solution. Any laws that regulate speech have the potential to become weapons that can be used by the party in power to accomplish anything they want to regardless of if it is something good or bad. Speech is a wildly variable medium of communication. Speech cannot be easily regulated objectively. Any attempt to do so quickly places society on a path towards dystopia. Each act of speech regulation erodes free speech. This goes on until we cannot say anything at all, which is something we need to avoid at all costs.

With that said, there are still actions that we, the American people, can take to resolve this issue. However, these actions are steps that we must take on an individual level together if we want to address the issue of hate speech in our society. The golden rule is an excellent place to start, where we "Do unto others as we would have done unto us." Much, if not all, of what qualifies as hate speech also happens to qualify as being unkind and, in many cases, ignorant and devoid of rational thought. If the speech we would speak is not the sort of speech we would want to hear about ourselves or our friends, then more often than not, we would be better off by not speaking it. This does not seem like a practical approach to addressing the issue of hate speech, but if we all lived by this rule, then the problem would be effectively solved.

Aside from exercising control over our own personal speech, we as a group, through the power of our republic and our capitalist economic system, could also go a long way toward addressing this issue through the use of our right to vote and our choice on where to spend our money. Politicians seem to be considered one of the larger sources of hate speech. We are the ones who ultimately determine the standards to which our politicians are held. If we choose to vote for candidates that hold themselves to a higher moral standard and avoid hate speech, then we can eliminate those candidates who lower themselves to an unbecoming level of speech. In the same way we can vote with election ballots, we can also vote with our dollars. In cases where hate speech takes place outside the realm of politics, we can individually choose to boycott those responsible for the hate speech. If enough people feel the same way about a situation such as this, then the combined effects of those boycotting will make an impact on the bottom line of those individuals perpetuating hate speech. The lost revenue acts as an excellent incentive to keep speech civil and free of hate.

Both of these alternatives fall on the road less traveled and will require a great effort on our part to bring about the desired results. If we make the collective choice to walk the path of being kinder to one another, we will most assuredly reap great rewards. Rewards that benefit us all, such as better interactions between each other and a stronger social fabric in general. The evening news would probably be a bit less depressing as well. Hate speech aside, it is time to get back to issues that our legislature can actually address without wrecking our society.

Second Edition Commentary:

Hate speech is probably the topic in this book that's gone the furthest downhill since the first edition release. In the last four years we've seen instances of big tech censorship being weaponized by political parties. Certain inflammatory individuals have been kicked off social media platforms entirely.

All actions on this front have been steps in the wrong direction. Instead of having people take responsibility and self-regulate, we've seen a lot of growth in the authoritarian approach to the problem. This is not a valid solution, and it has great potential for abuse. So far, we've witnessed the people holding the levers of power using them to beat down the people they disagree with.

This was especially rampant during the Covid era where anyone propagating "misinformation" was banned from public forms, demonetized, blacklisted, etc. At the current moment mid-2023, it looks like things are getting better on this front. This appears to be largely thanks to pushback by the masses and certain influential individuals.

Chapter 8: The Issue of Immigration

Background:

Once more starting with a definition, immigration is the act of coming to live permanently in a foreign country. Illegal alien, illegal immigrant, and unauthorized migrant are somewhat interchangeable, and all refer to a person in a country illegally. A visa is an official form of permission to enter, leave, or stay in a country. Usually, for a specific amount of time. Lastly, a green card is an authorization for a person to permanently live and work in the U.S.A. With those out in the open, we will now move on to our statistics for the issue.

Currently, around 43.3 million foreign-born people live in the United States [35]. Roughly 20.7 million of these people are U.S. Citizens, while the remaining 22.6 million people are not [35]. Of these 22.6 million non-citizens, around 13.1 million of them are lawful permanent residents, 1.7 million are temporary visa holders, and the remaining 11.1 million are unauthorized migrants [35]. For reference, the number of foreign-born people in the U.S. has increased considerably from just 9.6 million in 1965 to the current 43.3 million we have here today [35]. There has also been a shift in where the majority of these foreign-born people immigrate from. In 1960, 75% of immigrants to the U.S. were from European countries [35]. By 2015, this number had dropped to around 15% [35]. In 2015, immigration was much more diverse with 11.6 million immigrants originating from Mexico, 2.7 million from China, 2.4 million from India, 2 million from the Philippines, 1.4 million from El Salvador, 1.3 million from Vietnam, 1.2 million from Cuba and 1.1 million from both the Dominican Republic and South Korea [35]. Another noteworthy bit of information is that more Mexican immigrants are returning home than arriving in the United States. Between 2009 and 2014, 1 million immigrants returned to Mexico while only 870,000 entered the U.S., resulting in a net decrease [35].

With the statistics related to the number of immigrants entering and leaving the U.S. now laid out, we can get into the statistics that describe this immigrant population. In 2015, the number of women in the foreign-born population outnumbered the number of men, 51.4% to 48.6% [35]. 50.7% of immigrant household heads owned their own homes, for reference, the same homeownership statistic for U.S. born household heads is 65.2% [35]. The poverty rate for immigrants is 17.3%, which is higher than the 14.3% (the Census Bureau rate) poverty rate of U.S. born citizens [35]. Working class immigrant households use social programs such as Medicaid and Supplemental Security Income at similar or lower rates compared to native-born households [35].

It is undisputed that successful integration into American society improves the lives of immigrants. On average, immigrant children meet or exceed the educational attainment of third-plus generation U.S. citizens. This provides support to the notion that children of immigrants are often better off than their parents [35]. Second generation Americans in 2012 had a median annual household income of $58,100 which was $100 lower than the national average and higher than their parent's median annual household income of about $45,800 [35]. 36% of U.S. born children of immigrants are college graduates, which is 5% higher than the national average [35]. 11% of U.S. born children of immigrants live in poverty, which is below the national average poverty rate of 13% (the Pew Research rate) [35].

Focusing now on illegal immigration, specifically in 2007, the illegal immigrant population peaked at around 12.2 million, with immigrants from Mexico making up about half of that number [35]. In 2014, 42% of illegal immigrants were in the U.S. as a result of overstaying their visas, that percentage amounts to roughly about 4.5 million people [35]. From 2007 to 2014, 600,000 more people overstayed their visas than illegally crossed the border [35]. In 2014, around 21% of unauthorized immigrants lived in California, 15% lived in Texas, 8% lived in Florida, 7% lived in New York, 5% lived in New Jersey, and around 4% lived in Illinois [35]. The remaining 40% of unauthorized immigrants lived in the remaining 46 states.

Most unauthorized immigrants were long-term residents of the U.S., with the median length of residence being around 13.6 years in 2014 [35]. It is estimated that about 3 million unauthorized immigrants are living in the U.S. currently who could qualify for a green card. However, these unauthorized immigrants cannot adjust their immigration status without first leaving the country, which would make re-entry difficult [35]. Around 7 million individuals in the U.S. are living in mixed immigration status families. This means that they have family members who are illegal residents, legal citizens, and/or green card holders [35]. Lastly, in 2016, there were around 752,000 people who received a reprieve from deportation through the Deferred Action for Childhood Arrivals program or DACA.

Clearly, a substantial number of immigrants are living in the United States. Fortunately for us, the vast majority of these immigrants are here legally and are actively working and adding value to the economy. They have a substantial positive economic contribution. In 2016, it was estimated that immigrants added around $2 trillion to the U.S. GDP [35]. A 2010 analysis indicated that in that year, 90 of the Fortune 500 companies were founded directly by immigrants, and another 114 were founded by the children of immigrants [35]. Additionally, it is estimated that unauthorized immigrants contribute a net $12 billion to Social security, $35.1 billion to Medicare and $11.7 billion to state and local governments in the form of taxes [35].

The positive economic contributions of immigrants aside, let us look at the other side of the coin. Removing unauthorized immigrants could have a sizable negative impact on our economy. It is estimated that ending DACA could potentially cost the U.S.

$433.4 billion in GDP as well as decrease Social Security and Medicare contributions by $24.6 billion over the next 10 years [35]. Removing all unauthorized immigrants from the workforce could also lead to an estimated 2.6% GDP decline or an average annual loss of $434 billion [35]. This would amount to reducing the GDP by around $4.7 trillion over 10 years [35]. On top of this, mass deportation could also cost the federal government a substantial amount of lost revenue over the same period, with estimates placing the lost revenue at around $900 billion [35]. To provide a sense of scale, the average cost to deport a single person is around $10,070, which includes the cost of detainment, processing through immigration courts and then providing transportation out of the country [35]. So clearly, deportation is not a cheap process for the taxpayer.

Since we have discussed some of the major facts about the population distribution, contributions, and economic impacts of immigrants, there remains one more piece of the immigration puzzle. Now we will examine the process that immigrants must follow to become lawful residents of the United States. First things first, to temporarily enter the U.S., an individual must apply for a visa at a U.S. Embassy or a U.S. Consulate. However, if the entering individual is a citizen from one of the 38 countries that are participating in the Visa Waiver program, this step can be skipped [36]. A visa will allow a person to enter the U.S., but to become a permanent resident of the U.S., the process an individual must follow depends on if the individual is currently inside or outside of the United States.

If the individual is in the U.S., the first step in the journey to permanent residence is to apply for a Permanent Resident Card (also known as a Green Card) through the adjustment of status process. If the individual is outside the U.S., the first step is to apply for an immigrant visa through consular processing at a U.S. Embassy or U.S. Consulate abroad. After these first steps are complete, the next few steps of the process are largely the same regardless of location. In most cases, someone must sponsor the immigrating individual or file an immigration petition on behalf of the immigrating individual.

Once the immigration petition is approved, and a visa is available in the immigrating individual's category, the individual can then apply for either a green card or an immigration visa. Next, the immigrating individual will be required to undergo a medical examination. This examination is followed by an interview, which is then followed by the eventual decision on the applicant. Many people who journey to the U.S. enter through a family based or an employment-based visa. The family visa is based on the immigrant possessing a familial relationship with a U.S. citizen or permanent resident in the United States. The employment-based visa, on the other hand, generally requires a job offer from a U.S. based employer [36]. More information about the specifics of this process can be found at www.usa.gov/enter-us. With that, we have covered all of the basics required to enter the country and become a permanent resident.

From here, the path to U.S. citizenship is now open. To become a U.S. citizen, an individual must have had a Permanent Resident (Green) Card for at least five years if the individual is not the spouse of a U.S citizen. The individual must also be at least 18 years old. If these two requirements are met, then the individual can use the Department of Homeland Security U.S. Citizenship and Immigration Services M-480 Naturalization Eligibility Worksheet to determine if they are eligible to become a U.S. citizen. These are some examples of the requirements listed in the worksheet: being able to read, write and speak basic English, being a person of good moral character and knowing the fundamentals of U.S. history and the form and principles of the United States Government.

If the individual is eligible to become a U.S. citizen, then they can prepare and submit an N-400, Application for Naturalization form. After that, they will need to have a biometric screening and complete an interview. Once all of that is completed, the individual will eventually get a decision back on their N-400 form granting, postponing, or denying their naturalization. If the individual's N-400 form is accepted, then the individual will take an Oath of Allegiance to the United States and become a U.S. citizen. Much more information in far greater detail about the U.S. citizenship process can be found at https://www.uscis.gov/citizenship/learners/apply-citizenship.

This whole process is time-consuming, and it can also be costly. There are specific fees associated with each step of the process. Fortunately, the government does have policies in place to reduce or even remove some of the fees depending on the financial situation of the applicant. Looking at the different fees, from start to finish the whole process can cost an applicant somewhere between $4,000 and $11,000 depending on their circumstances. A safe bet for the average cost would be between $6,000 and $8,000. Without special consideration, uscis.gov currently lists the fee for Form N-400 alone at $725 if the cost of the biometric screening is included.

With that, we have discussed a good portion of the background information on this subject. Instead of discussing this process in greater depth, we will transition to discussing the Democratic stance on immigration.

The Stance on the Left: Amnesty and Free Immigration

Paraphrasing from the Democratic Party platform on immigration, the Democrats believe that the U.S. was founded as and continues to be a country of immigrants. They view immigration not as a problem to be solved but rather as a defining aspect of the American character. The Democratic Party supports legal immigration within a reasonable limit. They feel that immigration should meet the needs of families, communities, and the economy. They also think that our immigration policy should be maintaining the U.S.'s status as a beacon of hope for people seeking safety, freedom, and security. They feel that the current quota-based immigration system discriminates against certain immigrants. They feel that detention and deportation policies also discriminate against certain immigrants. They believe that we need to urgently fix our broken immigration system which "tears families apart and keeps workers in the shadows." Additionally, the Democratic Party thinks a path to citizenship for unauthorized law-abiding families who are already here in the United States needs to be created.

The Democratic Party believes that forced prolonged expulsion from the country as a consequence of an immigration law violation should be ended. They believe that the issue of family backlogs must be addressed. They also believe that the Deferred Action for Childhood Arrivals program and Deferred Action for Parents of Americans program must be maintained. They believe that there should not be religious tests to bar immigrants or refugees from entering the United States. Lastly, the Democratic Party believes that immigration enforcement should be focused on those who pose a threat to our country while also being humane in nature. They do not support raids or roundups of unauthorized immigrants. [25]

There is quite a bit to unpack there, but possible cynicism aside, the reasoning behind the Democratic stance on immigration would seem to be empathy. An argument could be made that a larger component of the Democratic base is comprised of immigrants when compared to Republicans, resulting in Democrats identifying more closely with immigrants when compared to Republicans. If we push this argument aside to the same place we drove our cynicism, then we are left with the conclusion that Democrats support immigration issues because they value human life and believe that immigrants make a positive contribution to our society.

They see immigrants as being people who have the potential to be great Americans. People who just want to make the most out of their lives and do what is best for their families. They also value the culture of immigrants. Democrats view it as a source of enrichment and not as a threat. With these views in mind, supporting immigration seems reasonable.

The Stance on the Right: Fair Legal Immigration

Switching to the other side of the issue and paraphrasing from the Republican Party platform on immigration, the Republicans are first and foremost thankful and supportive of legal immigrants who are contributing to American society. The Republican Party feels that immigration policy must serve the interests of the United States above all else. They are opposed to any form of amnesty for those who by breaking the law, have disadvantaged those who have obeyed the law by immigrating to the U.S. legally. The Republicans believe our highest priority should be to secure our borders and all ports of entry as well as enforcing our current immigration laws.

Some Republicans support the building of a border wall. Many Republicans support the enforcement of verification systems that prevent illegal immigrants from being able to work in the United States. They support stiffer penalties for illegal aliens who illegally re-enter the United States after having been deported before. The Republican Party also supports a more thorough vetting of refugees attempting to enter the United States. They do not support providing federal funding for sanctuary cities. [32] All of that more or less sums up the Republican perspective on immigration as they have it laid out in their party platform.

The Republican perspective on immigration is a bit more challenging to understand when compared to the Democratic perspective. Like Democrats, Republicans celebrate and support individuals legally immigrating to the United States. Individuals illegally entering the United States are a whole different matter. Once more putting cynicism aside, Republicans view these individuals as criminals who should be dealt with to the fullest extent of the law. They believe that these criminals are incapable of making positive contributions to our country and that they are a danger to American citizens. Instances where illegal immigrants commit high profile crimes (murder, rape, drug trafficking, etc.) only serve to reinforce these beliefs. On top of this, in some cases, there is also an underlying fear of illegal immigrants depriving Americans of jobs and abusing the welfare system. It is this fear that forms the core of the Republican stance on the issue of immigration. At the individual level, many Republicans are also afraid that illegal immigrants could hurt them, their family, or their way of life. They want to avoid this regardless of what it may cost.

The belief that we need to secure our borders stems from this desire for protection. Those who support building a border wall feel that a wall would be the best way to prevent unauthorized people from entering the country. To them, a wall is a commonsense solution to keep illegal people out of our country. This is perhaps a bit misguided since the largest component of unlawful immigrants in the country are here as a result of an overstayed visa, but it is nevertheless the default solution of a large component of the Republican base. Republicans support verification systems and stiffer penalties because these two things provide effective means to incentivize immigrants to immigrate legally.

If an individual cannot obtain a job in the U.S. upon arrival here, they have little incentive to remain here. Additionally, stiffer penalties such as a longer expulsion period make it much less attractive and much riskier to be in the U.S. illegally. Having discussed the views above, the lack of Republican support for sanctuary cities should make sense as well. The idea of certain cities harboring what are believed to be criminals would naturally be unappealing.

With that, we have more or less examined the core Republican views on immigration. Having done that, we can move forward and begin discussing possible compromises between both sides.

The Common Ground on The Issue of Immigration

As with most of the other issues we have discussed up to this point, the issue of immigration also has some common ground that both parties share. Both parties agree that legal immigrants are good for our economy. In the background section, we covered some of the data that outlines the exact contribution that immigrants, both legal and illegal, make to our economy. With that being the case, both parties should have no problem agreeing that having a larger number of skilled immigrants legally entering the country is a good thing for America.

Both parties can also agree that our current system for legal immigration has some major issues. One of the larger issues would be the amount of time that our immigration system requires to process immigration applicants along with the large backlog that has been created as a result. If the current immigration system was more efficient and user-friendly, it is likely that many of the unauthorized immigrants residing in the country would make an effort to gain legal status as opposed to taking risks associated with being in the U.S. illegally.

One potential solution to improve immigration efficiency that both parties should be able to support would be providing funding for a computer-based immigration system. With a computer-based system, immigrants would essentially be able to create an online immigration profile. They would then be able to upload all of the relevant paperwork, personal information, and reports to this single profile location. This would eliminate paperwork from the process, along with the need to track physical documents. This would also allow for the transfer of information to take place at the speed of the internet.

Aside from facilitating more efficient process tracking and information transfer, a computer-based system could also automate certain parts of the immigration process. Machine learning could be used to sort potential applicants into groups based on the amount of human interaction required for approval. Cases that would have a high likelihood of being approved could be fast-tracked to an approval phase, whereas cases that have more potential issues would be addressed by humans directly. If implemented, a system similar to the one described here would have the potential to save massive amounts of time and potentially pay for itself.

Another potential solution would be passing legislation that improves the processes required for immigrants to become American citizens. The current process is cumbersome, costly, and time-consuming. Both parties can agree that immigrants who quickly assimilate to American culture and positively contribute to our society are good for our country. Funding to make assimilation programs (English classes, American citizenship classes, and the like) more widely available to immigrants would go a long way towards accomplishing this end. Additionally, reducing the cost incurred by immigrants to become American citizens would also help facilitate the desire for immigrants to seek citizenship over remaining unauthorized.

The current high cost of citizenship effectively bars lower-income immigrants from being able to afford becoming citizens. The lifelong economic contributions and tax revenue generated by an American citizen are far greater than the comparatively minor contribution gained by charging immigrants a large amount of money to be granted residence and eventually citizenship status. The lifetime economic and tax contributions of an American citizen or of a legal permanent resident also far outweigh the economic and tax contributions of an unauthorized immigrant living in the United States. From a government standpoint, this also makes legal residency or citizenship a more favorable state for people residing within the United States.

One final compromised solution would be to provide a preferred citizenship process for immigrants that have a higher likelihood of positively contributing to American society. Immigrants who possess high demand skill sets, no criminal background, and the capability to pass a citizenship test could be given citizenship through a fast-track program. Such a program could have assimilation requirements, such as residing in the U.S. for a certain number of years after gaining citizenship, to ensure that such a fast-track system is not abused. A program like this would be based entirely on the facts and information provided by applicants, disregarding country of origin, religion, or any other discriminable trait. Since this kind of program would be unbiased and seeking the best and the brightest for America, both parties should be able to support it. A program like this could potentially ease a bit of the burden the current system is under.

The successful implementation of any of these compromises would undoubtedly improve our current immigration situation. Unlike other proposed solutions, such as building a border wall, these solutions have the potential to find support on both sides of the aisle, which is why we have outlined them here. With that said, we can now wrap up immigration and jump over to taxes.

Second Edition Commentary:
As of mid-2023, little progress has been made on the immigration front. The border remains unsecure. The immigration system hasn't seen major improvements. Most shockingly, the issue seems to have faded from the forefront of concern. That said, the first edition compromises still remain valid.

Chapter 9: The Issue of Taxes

Background:

Taxes, as defined by dictionary.com are, "a sum of money demanded by a government for its support or for specific facilities or services, levied upon incomes, property, sales, etc." This is probably the most unnecessary definition included so far since basically every single American over the age of 16 has had at least one experience with taxes. As most Americans are well aware, taxes can influence many life decisions such as employment, marriage, investment strategies, savings strategies, home ownership, and financing decisions. As a result, it is safe to say that taxes have a pretty significant impact on the lives of nearly all Americans.

With all of that said, we will start our discussion with some general information related to taxes. In 2016, tax revenue was $4.9 trillion, which breaks down to about $15,202 per person in the U.S. [37]. Adjusted for inflation, this tax per person figure has steadily increased from a low of $1,094 back in the 1920s and 30s to the current level [37]. Government spending has been on the rise, with spending outpacing tax revenue almost every year from the mid-1960s to the present [37]. The only exception to this trend was a short period in the late 1990s, during that time, tax revenue did increase faster than spending [37].

With supplementary materials included, the current federal tax code is around 10,000 pages long when printed on 8.5x11 inch paper with size 12 font [37]. If placed on a table, the federal tax code would stand about 19.7 inches (500 mm) tall, making it a fairly sizable and somewhat depressing stack of paper. Around 6.1 billion hours per year are spent complying with the requirements of federal tax laws [37]. In 2016, the IRS conducted a study that determined there was an average tax gap of about $406 billion between 2008 and 2010, which means that roughly 16.3% of taxes due over that period were not paid [37]. Also, on that note, willfully evading federal taxes is a felony crime that is punishable by up to 5 years in prison and fines up to $250,000 for individuals and $500,000 for companies [37]. Since taxes can be levied by all levels of government, we will now take a look at federal, state, and local taxes.

At the federal level, the U.S. government collected $3.3 trillion in taxes in 2016, which was 17.8% of the GDP or about $10,207 for each person living in the U.S. [37]. When broken up by source, 47% of federal taxes for 2016 came from the personal income tax, 37% from social insurance taxes, 11% from corporate income taxes, 3% from excise taxes, 1% from customs duties and 1% from estate and gift taxes [37].

In 2016 state and local governments collected $1.6 trillion in taxes, which was 8.7% of the U.S. GDP and amounted to $4,995 for each person living in the U.S. [37]. By source, 34% of these taxes came from sales tax, 29% from property taxes, 23% from personal income taxes, 4% from corporate income taxes, 1% from social insurance taxes and the remaining 8% from other assorted tax sources [37]. These figures together conclude our look at the high-level tax data that is readily available.

With the high-level tax data having been discussed, we can now turn our focus to those paying these taxes. Using 2013 numbers, the lowest 20% of households in the U.S. had an average household income of $25,400 and were taxed at an effective tax rate of 3.3%, which amounted to around $838 in taxes [37]. The next 20% of households in the U.S. had an average household income of $47,400 and were taxed at an effective rate of 8.4% or about $3,982 [37]. The middle 20% of households had an average income of $69,700 and were taxed at an effective rate of 12.8%, which was about $8,922 [37]. The fourth 20% of households had an average income of $103,700 and were taxed at an effective rate of 17% or about $17,629 [37]. The last 19% of households had an average household income of $265,000 and were taxed at an effective rate of 26.3% or about $69,695 [37]. The remaining 1% of households had an average income of $1,571,600 and were taxed at an effective rate of 34% or about $534,344 [37].

A few paragraphs above, we discussed the tax source breakdown for the different levels of the government. Now we will take a look at the exact nature of each one of those tax sources starting with the personal income tax. As one might have guessed, the personal income tax is a tax that is levied upon the income of an individual [37]. The personal income tax made up almost half of the taxes collected by the federal government [37]. Personal income taxes go towards the general fund of the U.S. Treasury. This means that the revenue generated by the personal income tax can be used for any legitimate purpose of government [37]. The personal income tax was initially proposed in 1913 with a bottom rate of 1% and a top rate of 7% [37]. For comparison, in 2016, the base rate was 10%, and the top rate was 39.6% however, this was just recently changed by tax reform legislation [37]. For the income tax, gross income is used in combination with some deductions and tax credits to determine a preliminary tax liability, which is taxed at certain rates as the size of income increases [37]. As a result, the income tax is known as a progressive tax system, since the tax rate increases as income increases.

Social insurance taxes make up the next major source of tax revenue. Social insurance taxes are levied to support programs like Social Security, Medicare, and unemployment insurance. In 2015, social insurance taxes made up 33% of the taxes collected by the federal government [37]. Both employers and employees pay social insurance taxes. However, employees usually bear the tax burden in the form of reduced wages. The tax burden of social insurance taxes is greater than the tax burden of income taxes for all groups except the top 20% of earners [37]. For some additional background, unemployment insurance started in 1936, Social Security began in 1937, and Medicare started in 1966 [37].

Excise and sales tax make up the next category of tax burdens we will look at. Sales tax is a tax that is placed on a wide range of goods and services. It must be paid each time a transaction occurs. Excise tax is a tax that is placed on a specific good or service only. Some examples of excise taxes would be the taxes placed on motor fuel, alcoholic beverages, tobacco products, firearms, air and ship transportation, certain environmentally hazardous activities and products, coal, telephone communications, certain types of gambling, and low fuel efficiency vehicles [37]. The excise tax is paid any time one of these items is purchased. To get a feel for the size of the excise tax burden, in 2013, the nationwide excise tax was estimated to be around $535 per person [37]. Moving back to sales tax, in 2015, sales tax made up 34% of the taxes collected by state and local governments [37]. As one might have guessed, the burden of these taxes fall mostly on consumers and those who purchase the goods that are subject to these taxes. Most often, the people affected the most by these taxes fall on the lower end of the income spectrum.

Next, on the list, property taxes are taxes that are levied on those who own taxable property such as land, buildings, or homes. Property taxes are most often levied by state and local governments. In 2015, property taxes made up 29% of state and local government tax revenue [37]. That year the nationwide average property tax was estimated to be around $1,439 per person [37]. Property taxes fall mostly on those who own land or homes. The yearly property tax for a given property is usually a percentage of that property's overall value. Many hospitals, colleges, and other non-profit organizations do not have to pay property taxes.

The final major tax category would be estate and gift taxes. The estate tax is imposed when someone transfers assets upon death. The gift tax is imposed when gifts are given. The gift tax is in place to prevent the estate tax from being avoided. Both taxes make up a small portion of federal tax revenue. As of 2018, up to

$15,000 can be gifted to any number of people without the transfer being subjected to the gift tax [38]. Once the $15,000 per person yearly limit is exceeded, there is an allowance that permits the giving of $11.2 million throughout a lifetime that is tax exempt. Money gifted beyond this $11.2 million is then taxed.

For more information or the complete background on U.S. tax law, consult the U.S. Tax code, which can be found at http://uscode.house.gov/download/download.shtml under title 26 - Internal Revenue Code. The pdf file has around 6,499 pages at the time of writing this. It is very long and somewhat painful to read. Since that is the case, we will limit the scope of our tax discussion to that which we have already covered in this background section. Instead of diving deeper into taxes, we will begin discussing the stances both parties hold on the matter.

The Stance on the Left: Tax the Wealthy

We will start by taking a look at the Democratic stance on taxes. To paraphrase this stance, the Democratic Party believes that the wealthiest Americans and the largest corporations should pay their fair share of taxes. The Democratic Party would like to remove tax breaks for companies that outsource jobs overseas. The same goes for oil and gas companies. The Democratic Party would also like to remove the methods that companies use to dodge their tax responsibilities. The Democratic Party would like to change the tax code to reward companies that invest in America and provide high-paying jobs in the U.S., not businesses that walk out on America. They would like to end tax deferrals, so U.S. Corporations pay U.S. taxes immediately on foreign profits. They would like to establish a multi-millionaire surtax to ensure that the wealthy pay their fair share. Additionally, they would like to shut down the "private tax system" and close loopholes. On top of all of these items, they would also like to offer tax relief to hard-working middle-class families. [25]

The reasoning behind the Democratic stance on taxes is very intuitive. They believe that everyone should pay their fair share. The catch here is that the Democratic Party believes that it is appropriate for the wealthy to pay a larger share of taxes than those who are not wealthy. In a way, this makes a bit of sense, at least at the individual level. After a person acquires a certain amount of wealth, additional wealth becomes a matter of extravagance instead of necessity. Essentially, the expenditure of wealth on required living expenses begins to make up a smaller and smaller portion of an individual's cash flow. Using this reasoning, a multi-millionaire can be taxed more without reducing the quality of his or her life when compared to a person who only has one thousand dollars to his or her name.

This same line of reasoning can be used on companies as well, however, in the case of companies, the money lost to taxes might be better used by the company than by the government. Companies tend to invest their excess money to grow their business. Using the money for the purpose of self-investment often generates more economic growth than the government would be able to generate if the money was collected through taxes instead.

The Democratic view that tax breaks need to end for oil companies and companies that outsource jobs also makes sense. Jobs that are moved out of our country result in reduced tax revenue for our government along with potentially weakening the economy. Since money for an outsourced job is being paid to a foreign citizen, it cannot be taxed like it would be if it were paid to an American. A foreign citizen is also less likely to spend the money on American products. This further detracts from the U.S. economy. As for oil companies, in this case, the Democratic Party wants to end oil company tax breaks on environmental conservation grounds. In their eyes, these tax breaks amount to rewarding oil companies for hurting our environment.

These two points aside, the remainder of the Democratic view on taxes is common sense. They want to reward companies who invest in our country and provide good jobs for Americans. Since these two actions benefit our nation, the Democrats want to provide positive reinforcement to promote these actions. They also want to eliminate tax loopholes for individuals and companies to prevent these groups from being able to avoid paying taxes. Lastly, their desire to offer tax relief to middle-class Americans would help improve the lives of many people in our country. This group of people also makes up a large pool of voters, so keeping middle-class America happy also serves the Democratic Party's best interests.

With that, we have covered the bulk of the Democratic stance on taxes. We can now transition to discussing the Republican position on taxes, which is a bit more restrained.

The Stance on the Right: Fair Taxes

Paraphrasing the stance on the right, the Republican Party believes that taxes are the biggest source of government influence on the economy. As a result of this belief, Republicans want to simplify the tax code and lower taxes that penalize thrift or discourage investment. Overall, Republicans want to change the sections of the tax code that are a disincentive for economic growth. On top of this, the Republican Party would like to eliminate special interest provisions, tax loopholes, and instances of corporate welfare. They are against taxes that deliberately divide Americans or promote class warfare. The Republican Party also believes that the creation of a value-added tax or a national sales tax must be tied to a simultaneous repeal of the federal income tax. [32]

The Republican stance on taxes is based on a different ideology than the Democratic stance. Generally speaking, the Republican Party holds the view that each individual is best suited to manage his or her own money. On top of this, they tend to believe that money in the hands of the people does a greater amount of good for the economy than money in the hands of the government. Added to this, the Republican Party also claims to support a small and limited government. These beliefs acting together form the justification for their tax stances.

They support a simplified tax code because it improves the quality of life for everyone involved with taxes. Since they believe that individuals and companies will spend their money more wisely than the government, it also follows that they want to have lower tax rates and eliminate taxes that would prevent people and companies from investing in the economy.

The three beliefs I mentioned earlier also play a role in Republicans wanting to eliminate tax loopholes, special interest tax provisions, and corporate welfare. All three of these practices cost the majority of taxpayers and benefit a few select groups. This amounts to using the government as a wealth distribution tool. It also misses the purpose of the government, which is to provide for the common good and to benefit everyone equally. Holding the belief that we are taxed enough the way it is, Republicans are opposed to additional taxes for that reason. And with that, we have more or less wrapped up the Republican stance on the issue of taxes.

The Common Ground on the Issue of Taxes

It is safe to say that all Americans dislike paying taxes. Both parties claim to support fair taxes, but the Republican definition of fair seems to be a bit different when compared to the Democratic definition of fair. Talking in terms of an income tax, taxing individuals at different tax rates is technically unfair regardless of how much wealth these individuals possess. The only fair tax would be a flat tax rate across the whole taxable population. In such a system, there would be no loopholes that could be exploited. Everyone would essentially pay a predetermined percentage of their income towards taxes. A tax system like this would be the fairest and the simplest to apply and enforce. All that an individual would need to do would be to take their taxable income and then multiply that number by the single flat tax rate to determine what their tax liability would be.

A tax system like this would save a massive amount of time for all of the parties involved with taxes. This sort of tax system would also most likely decrease the amount of taxes that go unpaid. A system like this would make it very difficult for an individual to dodge their tax liability once their income is known. Although a flat tax system would be the fairest, it would not be free of downsides. One such downside would be that we would need to arrive at a flat tax rate that would still bring in the same net tax revenue. That or the government could elect to spend less money, which would allow a slightly lower flat tax rate. However, at this point in the life of our nation the terms "government" and "spending less" can hardly be put together in the same sentence without it being considered the punchline to a joke.

Since the wealthy pay most of the taxes in our country, the taxes of the wealthy would probably go down a bit, while the taxes of the less wealthy would increase to arrive at our flat tax rate. A much larger component of the population would fall into the less wealthy category, so it is doubtful that there would be voter support for a tax change that would increase the tax liability for the majority of Americans. As a result, the only flat tax rate that would work would be using the lowest common denominator to borrow a math term. For 2018-2019 the lowest tax bracket rate was 10%. If our flat tax rate was lowered to this 10% rate for everyone across the whole country, then we could probably find voter support for such a change. However, that would amount to a major cut to the government's spending money. To put that into perspective, we can do a quick back of the envelope calculation. If the total taxable personal income in the U.S. is $17.5 trillion, a 10% income tax would give the government about $1.75 trillion to work with. This is a little over half of the 2016 federal tax revenue figure so it is clear that the 10% rate would fall short.

The only way forward with this tax rate would require the government to spend less or increase the spending deficit. As I mentioned before, the former option is unlikely at best, and the latter option of increasing our spending deficit is a horrible idea. So, all and all, it is pretty clear that a truly fair tax system is something our country will likely not see.

With a truly fair tax system off the table, we are left with the rose-colored versions of fairness that both parties hold a different opinion on. Given this different meaning of fairness, broad tax reform is most likely off the table. That does not mean we are out of options, though. There are a few points of interest that both parties can find agreement on that are related to taxes.

The first instance would be that tax loopholes are bad. Both parties state in their party platforms that they would like to eliminate tax loopholes that are exploited. As with the definition of fairness, both parties most likely have a different view of what constitutes a fair tax regulation and what would be considered a loophole. There should however be some degree of overlap between the two that would allow legislation to be drafted that could, in fact, improve the tax situation.

The other instance of platform agreement would be the sentiment that our current tax code is overly complicated. With this being the case, both parties should be able to find some common ground on legislation that can simplify the tax situation. One possible way to go about streamlining taxes would be passing legislation that modernizes the IRS. Another would be simplifying the tax deduction system or eliminating special tax circumstances. Any of these options have the potential to make the lives of millions of Americans much better.

Second Edition Commentary:

The first edition remains largely valid on the topic of taxes. Zero progress has been made on the tax front. We still have the overly complicated, loophole ridden, oppressive tax system we did in 2018. Making matters worse, the Federal Government has blown out spending beyond all possible comprehension.

As of writing this, the current national debt is about $32.07 trillion. The Federal Government spent about $6.5 trillion last year. With that kind of spending, there seems to be little interest or appetite for improving the tax system. This is unfortunately to the detriment of millions of Americans who have to deal with it on a yearly basis.

Chapter 10: The Issue of Government Size and Spending

Background:

This last issue is a pretty massive one. It is also closely related to our previous topic. Simply put, the U.S. government is enormous, there is little debate about this fact. Typically, when government size is considered, the discussion is in terms of government employees, the staggering number of laws and the amount of spending that takes place at the government's direction. All of these characteristics meaningfully describe the size of our government, so we will take a look at each one of them in our discussion.

Of these topics, we will start by looking at the number of individuals employed by the U.S. government. As most Americans will recall from high school, the U.S. government consists of three branches, known as the executive branch, the legislative branch, and the judicial branch. Each branch of the U.S. government employs a relatively large number of people. The executive branch employs a total of 2,674,353 civilians, with about 588,380 of those employees working for the Postal Service [39]. Additionally, the executive branch employs 1,352,081 individuals in the Department of Defense, 41,460 individuals in the Department of Homeland Security (USCG), 7,060 individuals in the Commissioned Corps (DOC, EPA, HHS), and then about 1,400,601 individuals who are serving in the military [39]. Adding all of these figures together provides a grand total of 4,074,954 individuals who are employed by the executive branch of the U.S. government [39]. Over time these employment numbers are likely to increase. The judicial and legislative branches are comparatively small, each employing 33,541 and 33,530 individuals, respectively [39]. That brings the total number of government employees up to 4,142,025 individuals [39].

To put that number into perspective, the U.S. government employs the same number of individuals as Walmart (2,300,000), Amazon (566,000), Yum China Holdings (450,000), Kroger (449,000) and Berkshire Hathaway (377,000) all added together [40]. For even more perspective, a little bit of math tells us that the U.S. government employs around 2.62% of the U.S. workforce if we use the 2016 Bureau of Labor Statistics to determine the size of our total workforce. The government is clearly massive in terms of the number of people employed.

Since we have discussed the size of the government workforce, let us now take a look at the legislative branch and their contribution to government size through the passage of laws. U.S. laws are categorized based on the intended purpose and placed under Titles which make up the United States Code, a codification of the general and permanent laws that govern our country. Currently, there are 54 Titles that make up the laws of the land, each about a different aspect of American life, with thousands of chapters that are filled to the brim with regulations. Of these 54 Titles, Title 53 is reserved and not in use. Some examples of Title categories would be General Provisions, Agriculture, Bankruptcy, and Education, which are the names for Title 1,7, 11 and 20, respectively.

Over the period between 1987 and 2017, Congress passed an average of 465.2 laws every year, further adding to the amount of content that is contained within the United States Code. In addition to passing laws, actions of the federal government that generate government agency rules, proposed rules, and public notices are recorded in the Federal Register, which acts as the official journal for the federal government. In 2013 there were 80,462 pages in the federal register. This large figure provides us with an idea of the amount of regulatory content that the federal government generates. [41] [42]

The second contribution the legislative branch makes to our government size would be through their control of the federal budget and how government funds are spent. In 2016, 63% of government spending was for social programs such as income security, healthcare, education, housing, and recreation [43]. 18% of spending was on national defense, which includes military spending along with veterans' benefits [43]. 14% of spending was for government and debt service, which included the executive and legislative branch spending, tax collection, financial management, and debt interest payment [43]. 4% of spending went to economic affairs, which included transportation, general economic & labor affairs, agriculture, natural resources, energy, and space exploration [43]. The remaining 1% of spending was spent on public order and safety, which includes spending on police, fire, legal courts, prisons, and immigration enforcement [43].

Jumping to 2018, as of September 30th, the U.S. government had a financial year obligated spending amount of $6.6 trillion. The breakdown of this spending is as follows: $1.1 trillion on Medicare (16%), $1.0 trillion on Social Security (15.7%), $1.0 trillion on National Defense (15.7%), $656.4 billion on Health (9.9%), $548.4 billion on Income Security (8.3%), $535.1 billion on Net Interest (8.1%), $432.2 billion on General Government (6.5%), $205.6 billion on Veterans Benefits and Services (3.1%), $132.2 billion on Internal Affairs (2%), $129.450 billion on Education, Training, Employment, and Social Services (2%), $116.2 billion on Transportation (1.8%), $84.6 billion on Community and Regional Development (1.3%), $77.0 billion on Natural Resources and Environment (1.2%) $76.5 billion on Administration of Justice (1.2%), a combined total of $141.9 billion on Commerce and Housing Credit, General Science, Space and Technology, Agriculture and Energy (2.1%) [43]. On top of all of this spending, an additional $339.1 billion has been listed as unreported (5.1%) and not currently accounted for [43].

A diligent reader might remember from the last chapter that these government spending totals exceed the amount of money that the federal government gathers from taxes over a year. As a result, this level of spending creates a deficit and results in the creation of a substantial amount of debt.

As of October 4, 2018, the official debt of the U.S. government was $21.6 trillion (at one point $21,599,377,345,082 to be exact), which is $65,710 for every living person in the U.S., $171,119 for every household, 106% of the U.S. GDP and 623% of the annual federal tax revenue [44]. This debt does not account for all financial liabilities the U.S. government is responsible for. At the end of the 2017 fiscal year, an additional $9.2 trillion was owed in the form of federal employee retirement benefits, accounts payable, and environmental/disposal liabilities [44]. $30.8 trillion was held in obligations to current Social Security participants above and beyond projected revenues from payroll and benefit taxes, certain transfers from the general fund of the U.S. treasury, and assets of the Social Security trust fund [44]. On top of that, an additional $34.6 trillion was held in obligations for current Medicare participants above and beyond projected revenues from payroll taxes, benefit taxes, premium payments, and the assets of the Medicare trust fund [44]. Combining all of these figures results in a total obligation of $88.9 trillion which amounts to $272,405 for every living person in the U.S., $704,391 for every U.S. household, 456% of the U.S. GDP and 2,485% of current annual federal tax revenues [44]. All of that said, these figures are based on current laws and do not account for future costs of other existing or new policies [44].

These are incomprehensibly large numbers, so to add a small bit of perspective, with the October 2018 debt, a person could buy 1,661.5'ish Gerald R. Ford-class nuclear-powered aircraft carriers [45]. A person could also buy 11,175,497 square miles of U.S. farmland valued at $3,020 per acre which is 3.04 times the land area of the U.S. and only about 3.42 million square miles short of the surface area of the moon [46]. Lastly, with that much money, at October 25th, 2018 prices, a person could buy a perfect cube of solid gold that would stand 100 feet high (99.9 ft to be exact) and weigh around 600,892 tons, which is 2.91 times the estimated amount of gold that has ever been mined [47] [48].

This massive amount of debt is currently owned by several different entities. In September of 2017 31% of the national debt was held by foreign and international entities, 29% was owned by domestic non-federal entities, 28% was owned by federal government funds and the remaining 12% was owned by the Federal Reserve [44].

The mountain of debt aside, as the size of the government increases, the efficiency of the government tends to decrease. Many Americans are familiar with countless stories about the smothering bureaucracy that is encountered in dealings with the Department of Transportation or the IRS. In the worst of these stories, a simple task is often drawn out into a time-consuming nightmare.

The U.S. government accountability office lists many potential improvements that the government could enact to reduce the amount of waste that is present. Some examples are having the Department of Defense minimize overlap in U.S. distribution centers for troop support, having the Department of Energy adopt alternative low activity radioactive waste storage, having the VA adopt supply practices used by leading hospitals to improve supply chains, having the Coast Guard close unneeded boat stations or having Congress and the IRS use more online systems to conduct business. [49]

The Stance on the Left: Mixed

A look at the Democratic Party platform reveals a mixed stance on government size and spending. On the whole, the Democratic Party supports spending on Social Security. They make that much clear in their party platform. Quoting from their party platform, they say that, "We will fight every effort to cut, privatize, or weaken Social Security, including attempts to raise the retirement age, diminish benefits by cutting cost-of-living adjustments, or reducing earned benefits." [25] In general, the Democratic Party stance is often oversimplified. It is assumed that they support spending on the majority of social programs, although this is not outlined in their party platform.

The Democratic Party does realize that the national debt is a problem and that we, as a nation, need to keep our spending in check. Quoting from their party platform, "We [the Democratic Party] will also ensure that new spending and tax cuts are offset so that they do not add to the nation's debt over time. We will tackle waste, fraud, and abuse to make sure government dollars are spent wisely and efficiently." [25] Overall, it is a bit unclear how they will go about offsetting new spending and tax cuts to create a balanced budget. They provide much more information on how they will go about increasing government efficiency but do not say much about how they will balance the budget.

Directly quoting from their party platform, "... Democrats will make government simpler and more user-friendly. The federal government too often operates with websites designed from another era that are too complicated, too hard to use, and rarely designed for mobile phones or tablets. We will build on the creation of the United States Digital Service (USDS) and give it the resources it needs to transform and digitize the top 25 federal government programs that directly serve citizens. We will eliminate internal barriers to government modernization. And we will use technology to improve outcomes and government accountability by embracing prioritized goal setting and performance tracking for the federal government." [25] From this, it is clear that the Democratic Party views technology as the way forward to improve government efficiency, but there is still little information in the Democratic Party platform that indicates how they will address the fraud and waste issues with our government.

The exception to this would be spending that is related to the military, which the Democratic Party addresses in their party platform. Quoting from the platform, "We must end waste in the defense budget. We will audit the Pentagon, launch a high-level commission to review the role of defense contractors, and take greater action against those who have been involved in fraud. And we will ensure that the Department of Defense invests its budget wisely." [25] In this case, they describe the actions they would take to eliminate spending waste, but really do not outline a plan for how they would address waste in the other branches of our government.

Overall, the Democratic stance stems from a belief that our large government, along with its corresponding social programs, are a net benefit to society. They believe that both provide a benefit that is greater than the cost. The Democratic Party holds the belief that our society runs more smoothly when there are adequate government officials to direct the affairs of our citizens. Additionally, they hold the belief that our social programs positively contribute to a great enough number of Americans to make them worth their cost to taxpayers. Since there is not much that needs to be added to this, we can transition to the Republican stance on this issue.

The Stance on the Right: Get Rid of Social Programs

The Republican Party is concise with its approach to government size and spending. Paraphrasing from the Republican Party platform, they believe that a firm cap should be placed on future debt. Along with such a cap, they also believe that we need to reaffirm principles of a responsible and limited government, similar to what we had in the early days of our union. On the whole, they want to restrain spending and are opposed to government expansion on spending and benefits for preferred groups. They believe that there should be a constitutional requirement for a balanced federal budget and that thrift should be prioritized over extravagance. In fewer words, the Republican Party believes that the taxpayer should be put first.

The Republican Party is against the current Medicare and Social Security programs because of the cost that these programs place on younger Americans who simply will not be able to support the increasing number of beneficiaries in the coming years. Additionally, the Republican Party supports appropriate defense spending. Beyond this, the Republican Party platform does not meaningfully address the issue of spending. [32]

The argument for a small and limited government did not originate with the Republican Party, but they do claim to support it. The argument essentially encompasses a few ideas. The first idea is that individuals can manage their personal and business affairs better than the government can. The second idea is that the government should only be used to provide common benefits for all citizens. The last idea is that in most cases, the efficiency of the government decreases as the size of the government increases. These three premises make intuitive sense and are easy to demonstrate. The vast majority of individuals would agree that they feel better suited than their parents or close friends to decide how to spend their money, where to go to college, where to live, what occupation to pursue, who to marry and what to do with their lives. If people, in general, feel like they can direct their lives better than a close friend could, it is no wonder that they would not want impartial government officials making these choices for them.

Presently it does not seem like the government has any control over these things, but through tax laws, scholarships, grants, and general regulations, the government can greatly influence these choices for individuals. Individual affairs aside, the idea that the government should only be used to provide common benefits to all is also straightforward to understand.

Paying taxes in exchange for services that provide a benefit to oneself can be considered a fair trade. Paying taxes to fund the local fire station makes sense because at some point the fire station might benefit all individuals in that fire district. However, paying taxes that end up getting used for the benefit of only a select group of people essentially amounts to stealing. Since I have used this example a few times by now, hopefully, we all can agree that stealing is morally wrong.

If that much is not clear, here is a better example. If a given individual realized that their neighbor was starving, he or she might willingly give his or her neighbor some money to use to get food. However, if a random third party showed up and took some money at gunpoint from the individual in question and then proceeded to give that money to the neighbor, feelings might be different. It is very likely that the individual would be pretty unhappy with being robbed on his neighbor's behalf even though the end result would be the same as when he volunteered the money. This principle is essentially what using tax money to benefit select groups amounts to.

The last of the three ideas I listed is also rather intuitive and requires little explanation. Without taking proactive measures to improve efficiency, as an organization grows larger more people tend to be involved with the decision-making process. More time is spent on communication and ensuring everyone is on the same page. The end result is that the organization becomes less efficient and more cumbersome as it grows in size. This is often also associated with cost increases as well. So overall, these three ideas are a big part of what the Republican Party bases their negative stance on government size upon. Having discussed both sides, we can now move on to our final compromise discussion.

The Common Ground on the Issue of Government Size and Spending

There is a good deal of compromise to be made on the issue of government size and spending. Both parties claim to be opposed to waste; however, both sides also seem to have a different set of criteria for what constitutes waste. They also differ in what would be considered mandatory spending. For the Democratic Party, a large amount of military spending seems to be classified as wasteful, whereas Republicans view military spending as necessary. For the Republican Party, a large amount of the spending on social programs seems to be considered wasteful as well, whereas Democrats view social program spending as crucially important to citizens. Like usual, it would seem like both parties are directly opposed yet again, fortunately for us, that is not entirely the case. There are still a few legislative actions that can be taken, on which both parties should be able to agree.

One example can be taken directly from the Democratic Party platform. Inefficiencies in many federal programs or federal agencies such as the IRS could be addressed by adopting computerized systems. Websites could be improved and made much more user-friendly and easier to navigate as well. As outlined in their platform, the Democrats would like to implement this sort of change to the top 25 federal programs that citizens interact with. However, improvements could be applied to many other areas as well. The Republican Party has no reason to oppose this sort of change, so any legislative action limited in scope to providing funding and a directive to computerize federal programs and update their user interfaces should be able to pass even through a divided Congress.

Both parties agree that a more user-friendly and straightforward government would be an improvement over our current governmental situation. Therefore, both parties should be able to recognize that creating legislation that is simpler and less convoluted would be better for everyone involved in American politics. This could be accomplished by placing a limit on the length of bills while also requiring them to be written in common everyday language. Additionally, the combination of multiple bills into giant bill packages could be prohibited, which would further simplify things. As it currently stands, many of these bill packages are never fully read or understood by the representatives that are voting on them, much less the members of the general public that are affected by these laws. Another possible improvement would be if Congress made an effort to repeal existing regulations that are no longer applicable or productive. If we continue to use an additive legislative system, as time goes on, we will eventually reach a point where we are bound by more laws than any person could learn in a lifetime of legal study.

These changes I have just outlined would not even require legislative action to implement. Our representatives could decide to only introduce simplified and concise legislation going forward. That would be the high road, which they should be willing to take if they genuinely want to improve the quality of their governance. However, it is unlikely that they would do this without significant pressure from us, their constituents. Most likely, if we want this sort of change, we will need to provide our representatives with an incentive to keep it short and simple. The best incentive would be our votes, in my opinion, but other incentives might work as well.

Both parties claim that they do not want to continue increasing the national debt. However, neither party seems willing to take any action to prevent the continued accumulation of debt every year. There are many excuses from both sides of the aisle to explain this lack of action. These excuses aside, if both parties are genuinely against continually generating more debt, then they should be able to support a major change that would prevent the continual generation of more debt. Such a change would be a law or a constitutional amendment that would require the government to have a balanced budget where government spending does not exceed government revenue unless there is a national emergency. The most basic and fundamental piece of financial wisdom is to spend less than you earn. Those individuals who follow this rule usually find some degree of success in life, and the same rule can be applied not only to a household but also to a much larger organization such as the federal government.

As it currently stands, we, tax-paying American citizens, are paying billions of dollars a year to cover the interest on the national debt. If the national debt was smaller or eliminated altogether, these billions of dollars could be saved in the form of a tax break or be used to fund other programs that actually provide a benefit to Americans. If our representatives really do care about the future of our country, then they would take the national debt more seriously and realize that we need to begin dealing with our debt load before it becomes large enough to crush us.

Second Edition Commentary:
Little needs to be said on this topic. The first edition aged well, and all the remarks on this topic ring true. Government size and spending has only gotten worse in the last four years. There are no signs of improvement on the horizon. The only hope we have is a monetary crisis forcing the issue upon us and forcing us to solve the issue. Otherwise, it will continue to go unchecked.

Final Remarks

We have now reached the end of our discussion on a few of the political issues facing America. As I said in the preface, it was my goal to save you some time in your quest to become better informed. With any luck, I accomplished that much, and you found the topics we have discussed informative. Our list of topics included some of the most divisive issues facing America. Yet despite this, we were able to take a look at some compromises for each of those issues. Our ability to do this shines more light on the underlying issue that we talked about in chapter 1. More often than not, the fights and disagreements we find ourselves in are a result of a failure to communicate and understand the other side instead of being the result of an actual lack of a solution.

As you move forward in life, I hope you will keep that much in mind. Especially the next time you run across a person who holds different political views than your own. These are the encounters you have control over. Paraphrasing from a Jordan Peterson YouTube lecture I watched a while back; we must first put our own house in order before we begin to criticize what is wrong in the world. Something similar is also said by Stephen Covey in *The 7 Habits of Highly Effective People*. Jesus also said something similar in the book of Matthew 7:5, "… first, remove the plank out of your own eye, and then you will see clearly to remove the speck from your brother's eye." Once again paraphrasing, both advise us to focus on what we can exercise control over, namely ourselves.

Although the issues we have discussed affect our nation at the national level, the changes we can make individually are found at the personal level and demonstrated in our interpersonal interactions. Separately the impact we have on our country as individuals can be somewhat limited. But if we all focus on improving the quality of our personal and interpersonal interactions, then the cumulative effect will be enough to impact our country.

With that, I will put down my pen. I wish you the best of luck in your future endeavors and hope you will continue to take steps to enrich your own life and the lives of others.

Citations/Sources

[1] FAQ About Genetic and Genomic Science. (2018, September 7). Retrieved January 2, 2019, from https://www.genome.gov/19016904/faq-about-genetic-and-genomic-science/

[2] Grimes, D. A. (2005). Risks of Mifepristone Abortion In Context. *Contraception,71*(3), 161. doi: Grimes DA. Risks of mifepristone abortion in context. Contraception. 2005;71:161

[3] Bartlett, L. A., MD, MHSc, Berg, C. J., MD, MPH, Shulman, H. B., MS, Zane, S. B., DVM, Green, C. A., MD, MPH, Whitehead, S., MD, MPH, & Atrash, H. K., MD, MPH. (2004). Risk Factors for Legal Induced Abortion-Related Mortality in the United States. *Obstetrics & Gynecology,104*(3), 635. doi: 10.1097/01.AOG.0000116260.81570.60

[4] Reproductive Health. (2018, August 07). Retrieved January 3, 2019, from https://www.cdc.gov/reproductivehealth/maternalinfanthealth/pregnancy-mortality-surveillance-system.htm

[5] Jatlaoui TC, Shah J, Mandel MG, et al. Abortion Surveillance — United States, 2014. MMWR Surveill Summ 2017;66(No. SS-24):1–48. DOI: http://dx.doi.org/10.15585/mmwr.ss6624a1.

[6] Induced Abortion in the United States. (2018, January 31). Retrieved January 3, 2019, from https://www.guttmacher.org/fact-sheet/induced-abortion-united-states?gclid=CjwKCAjw7tfVBRB0EiwAiSYGMycmcNdWA_0kAT75HTYdxqtVcoF_ulQ23GUcN6hmyRp3bQaSSY_OLBoCVvMQAvD_BwE

[7] Democratic Party on Abortion. (2018, September 11). Retrieved January 3, 2019, from http://www.issues2000.org/celeb/Democratic_Party_Abortion.htm

[8] Republican Party on Abortion. (2018, September 11). Retrieved January 3, 2019, from http://www.ontheissues.org/Celeb/Republican_Party_Abortion.htm

[9] Parenthood, P. (n.d.). Birth Control Methods & Options | Types of Birth Control. Retrieved January 3, 2019, from https://www.plannedparenthood.org/learn/birth-control

[10] Martinez, G., Ph.D., Abma, J., Ph.D., & Copen, C., Ph.D. (2010, September). Educating Teenagers About Sex in the United States. Retrieved January 3, 2019, from https://www.cdc.gov/nchs/data/databriefs/db44.pdf

[11] NASA. (2005). *NASA - What's the Difference Between Weather and Climate?*. [online] Available at https://www.nasa.gov/mission_pages/noaa-n/climate/climate_weather.html [Accessed 5 Jan. 2019]

[12] Haigh, J. (2003). The effects of solar variability on the Earth's climate. *Philosophical Transactions of the Royal Society of London. Series A: Mathematical, Physical and Engineering Sciences*, 361(1802), pp.95-111.

[13] Lindsey, R. (2018, August 01). Climate Change: Atmospheric Carbon Dioxide. Retrieved January 28, 2019, from https://www.climate.gov/news-features/understanding-climate/climate-change-atmospheric-carbon-dioxide

[14] Climate Change: Vital Signs of the Planet. (n.d.). Retrieved January 5, 2019, from https://climate.nasa.gov/

[15] Climate Change Indicators: U.S. Greenhouse Gas Emissions. (2016, December 17). Retrieved January 5, 2019, from https://www.epa.gov/climate-indicators/climate-change-indicators-us-greenhouse-gas-emissions

[16] U.S. Primary Energy Consumption by Source and Sector In 2017. (n.d.). Retrieved January 5, 2019, from https://www.eia.gov/energyexplained/index.cfm?page=electricity_in_the_united_state

[17] Environment. (2016). Retrieved January 5, 2019, from https://democrats.org/issues/environment/

[18] Party Platform. (2016). Retrieved January 5, 2019, from https://democrats.org/about/party-platform/#climate-justice

[19] Republican National Committee. (2016). Retrieved January 5, 2019, from https://www.gop.com/platform/americas-natural-resources/

[20] The NCES Fast Facts Tool provides quick answers to many education questions (National Center for Education Statistics). (n.d.). Retrieved January 5, 2019, from https://nces.ed.gov/fastfacts/display.asp?id=372

[21] Carnevale, A. P., Smith, N., & Strohl, J. (n.d.). *Recovery* [PDF]. Washington D.C.: Georgetown University.

[22] Digest of Education Statistics, 2016. (n.d.). Retrieved January 5, 2019, from

https://nces.ed.gov/programs/digest/d16/tables/dt16_330.10.a
sp?current=yes

[23] Woodhouse, K. (2015, June 12). Impact of Pell Surge.
Retrieved January 5, 2019, from
https://www.insidehighered.com/news/2015/06/12/study-us-
higher-education-receives-more-federal-state-governments

[24] Democratic Party on Education. (2018, September 11).
Retrieved January 5, 2019, from
http://www.ontheissues.org/celeb/Democratic_Party_Education
.htm

[25] Party Platform. (2016). Retrieved January 5, 2019, from
https://www.democrats.org/party-platform

[26] Republican Party on Education. (2018, September 11).
Retrieved January 6, 2019, from
http://www.ontheissues.org/Celeb/Republican_Party_Educatio
n.htm

[27] Thomas, S. (2018, November 29). Statistics on Drug Addiction.
Retrieved January 6, 2019, from
https://americanaddictioncenters.org/rehab-guide/addiction-
statistics

[28] State GDP Data from
https://apps.bea.gov/iTable/iTable.cfm?0=1200&isuri=1&reqid=
70&step=10&1=1&2=200&3=sic&4=1&5=xx&6=-1&7=-1&8=-
1&9=70&10=levels#reqid=70&step=10&isuri=1&7003=200&7035=
-1&7004=naics&7005=1&7006=xx&7036=-
1&7001=1200&7002=1&7090=70&7007=-1&7093=levels

[29] Substance Abuse and Mental Health Services Administration. (2018). Key substance use and mental health indicators in the United States: Results from the 2017 National Survey on Drug Use and Health (HHS Publication No. SMA 18-5068, NSDUH Series H-53). Rockville, MD: Center for Behavioral Health Statistics and Quality, Substance Abuse and Mental Health Services Administration. Retrieved from https://www.samhsa.gov/data/

[30] Wagner, P., & Sawyer, W. (2018, March 14). Mass Incarceration: The Whole Pie 2018. Retrieved January 6, 2019, from https://www.prisonpolicy.org/reports/pie2018.html

[31] Prison Spending in 2015. (n.d.). Retrieved January 6, 2019, from https://www.vera.org/publications/price-of-prisons-2015-state-spending-trends/price-of-prisons-2015-state-spending-trends/price-of-prisons-2015-state-spending-trends-prison-spending

[32] *Republican Platform 2016*[PDF]. (2016). Republican Party. from https://prod-cdn-static.gop.com/static/home/data/platform.pdf

[33] Be Informed: Gun Control Just Facts. (n.d.). Retrieved January 6, 2019, from https://www.justfacts.com/guncontrol.asp

[34] Hate Speech and Hate Crime. (2017, December 12). Retrieved from http://www.ala.org/advocacy/intfreedom/hate

[35] Nicholson, M. D., & CAP Immigration Team. (2017, April 20). The Facts on Immigration Today: 2017 Edition. Retrieved January 6, 2019, from https://www.americanprogress.org/issues/immigration/reports/2017/04/20/430736/facts-immigration-today-2017-edition/

[36] How to Enter the U.S. (n.d.). Retrieved January 6, 2019, from https://www.usa.gov/enter-us

[37] Be Informed: Taxes Just Facts. (n.d.). Retrieved January 6, 2019, from https://www.justfacts.com/taxes.asp

[38] TurboTax. (2018). The Gift Tax. Retrieved January 6, 2019, from https://turbotax.intuit.com/tax-tips/estates/the-gift-tax/L1sFpFeXV

[39] Jennings, J, & Jared, N. (2018). *Federal Workforce Statistics Sources: OPM and OMB* (CRS Report No. R43590). Retrieved from Congressional Research Service website:https://fas.org/sgp/crs/misc/R43590.pdf

[40] Fortune 500 Companies 2018: Who Made the List. (n.d.). Retrieved January 6, 2019, from http://fortune.com/fortune500/list/filtered?sortBy=employees&first500

[41] http://uscode.house.gov/browse/&edition=prelim

[42] Statistics and Historical Comparison. (n.d.). Retrieved January 6, 2019, from https://www.govtrack.us/congress/bills/statistics

[43] US Gov Spending Explorer FY 2018 Obligated Amount. (n.d.). Retrieved January 6, 2019, from https://www.usaspending.gov/#/explorer/budget_function

[44] Be Informed: National Debt Just Facts. (n.d.). Retrieved January 6, 2019, from https://www.justfacts.com/nationaldebt.asp

[45] O'Rourke, R. (2018). *Navy Ford (CVN-78) Class Aircraft Carrier Program: Background and Issues for Congress* (CRS Report No. RS20643). Retrieved from Congressional Research Service website:https://fas.org/sgp/crs/weapons/RS20643.pdf

[46] Farmland Value Guide. (2015, August). Retrieved January 6, 2019, from https://www.agweb.com/land/farmland-value-guide/

[47] Gleason, S. (2018, March 07). Gold Spot Price Per Ounce Today, Live & Historical Charts in USD. Retrieved January 6, 2019, from https://www.moneymetals.com/precious-metals-charts/gold-price as priced on **10/25/2018**

[48] How much gold has been mined? (2017, December 14). Retrieved January 6, 2019, from https://www.gold.org/about-gold/gold-supply/gold-mining/how-much-gold

[49] Dodaro, G. L. (2018). *Government Efficiency and Effectiveness: Opportunities to Reduce Fragmentation, Overlap, and Duplication and Achieve Other Financial Benefits*. U.S. Government Accountability Office. doi: GAO-18-498T from https://www.gao.gov/assets/700/691505.pdf

About the Author

Chandler Rivinius grew up in a small town in Midwest America. He had a pleasant childhood, thanks to his wonderful parents. Upon graduating from high school, he attended college for an engineering degree. After graduating from college, Chandler applied to and got hired by a manufacturing company in a design engineering capacity. In his free time, he enjoys playing the piano, being outdoors, reading a wide variety of books, staying active, and spending time with friends and family. He is passionate about science, learning, his Christian beliefs, and having a positive impact on the world around him.